Centerville Library
Washington-Centerville Public Library
Centerville, Ohio

DISCARD

W9-ACI-669

LOVE YOUR LUNCH

COOKBOOK

LOVE YOUR LUNCH COOKBOOK

SEAN WAINER

Photography by
Salka Hamar Penning

MURDOCH BOOKS
SYDNEY · LONDON

Contents

Introduction

Growing up in Melbourne, I have been around food more or less all my life. When I was seventeen, my mother took over a health-food store with a take-away food section that had not been doing very well, but she saw its potential. She put the last of her savings into every appliance you could imagine, from a frozen yoghurt maker to pie warmers. We pimped up the menu with our homemade falafel in pita bread with hummus and fresh tabouleh: a big success!

My culinary journey continued when I was twenty, and I started travelling. In Chianti, Italy, I had the good fortune to live with a lovely lady, my friend's mother. She was an amazing cook and she loved to take me with her around the markets. I would watch her with admiration as she carefully chose the perfect tomato and just the right cheese. I realised then that good cooking is not just making a meal in a kitchen. It's about knowing and selecting the best of every ingredient to make as perfect a dish as possible.

After Italy came Amsterdam. I worked as a cook in a variety of cafés and restaurants before starting Small World Catering in 1999. Little did I know that within a year Small World would become a successful catering business and a bustling café. The menu burst with gourmet sandwiches, take-home meals, fresh salads, pressed juices and, of course, great coffee. Located on a really sunny street corner with spare crates as seating, Small World's terrace was born and our popularity grew.

All the knowledge I've acquired over the years culminates in Small World, but it's the people who have made the shop what it is today. It's almost impossible to estimate the number of nationalities that have worked with me over the years. They have come to Small World from all over the globe, from Russia and Africa, Iceland to America. Each one of them bringing his or her own twist to the dishes. Quite a few of those dishes are still with us today: the Spanish Tortilla, French Lemon Tart, New York Cheesecake, Thai Fish Cakes, Mediterranean Couscous and the Mexican Burritos. Over the years, Small World has become an Amsterdam institution, featuring in loads of magazines and travel guides. The locals think of Small World as 'their' place, as do regular visitors to Amsterdam, who always stop in when they're in town for a bite and a chat. This book has long been a wish of mine, now realized thanks to a loyal customer who wanted to help make it happen for years. Her favourite is the berry muffin!

Love your Lunch is not only a book about Small World. It is, most of all, a book about home-cooked comfort food served with an elegant twist. I want to show you how to make delicious lunches using the best ingredients and the simplest techniques. The recipes have all been tried and tested, not just by our own chefs, but also by people without a chef's experience. They work, and they are delicious. We put every recipe we could fit in into Love your Lunch, including our famous Carrot Cake. It was hard to give that one away, but it wouldn't be the Small World cookbook without it!

Sauces, Spreads AND OTHER Stuff You'll Need

The sauces and spreads you'll find here freeze well. This is very handy when you have leftovers, or when you need to save time during the week, as you can prepare ahead. They still taste perfect!

Coriander Hummus

Small World hummus is a bit chunky, not creamy.

Method

Place the chickpeas in a large bowl and cover with double their quantity of water. Leave to soak overnight. Drain, rinse, and transfer to a large saucepan. Add water, bring to the boil, reduce the heat, and simmer 1 1/2 hours, or until the chickpeas are cooked but still have some bite. Avoid mushy chickpeas.

Put the garlic cloves, tahini paste and cumin into a food processor, and pulse to mix. Add the coriander and lemon zest, and give it a whirl. Add the chickpeas, and blitz it until you have a coarse mixture, not entirely smooth. Then, slowly drizzle in the olive oil until it's the consistency you like. At Small World, we keep its texture on the coarse side. Finish off with salt and pepper to taste.

Ingredients

250 g (9 oz) dried chickpeas
4 garlic cloves, peeled
150 g (5 1/2 oz) tahini paste, measured after stirring
1 teaspoon ground cumin
1/2 handful fresh coriander (cilantro), leaves and stalks
1 tablespoon lemon zest
100 ml (3 1/2 fl oz) extra-virgin olive oil, or more if needed
sea salt and black pepper

Lemon Olive Oil

This sauce is a great basis for so many of our dishes as it gives any sandwich a kick. You can make it in advance and store it for weeks in the fridge. Since we're using the skin of the fruit here, organic lemon is your best choice.

Ingredients

500 ml (17 fl oz) good-quality extra-virgin olive oil
4 lemons, preferably organic and unwaxed,
juiced, and zest cut into thin strips
1 teaspoon dried oregano
1 teaspoon dried chilli flakes

Method

Pour the olive oil into a small, heavy saucepan and place over the lowest heat possible. Add the lemon zest, oregano and chilli flakes. The lemon zest will slowly rise to the surface of the olive oil as it reaches the right temperature. Turn off the heat at this point, strain the oil, discard the lemon zest, and set aside to cool. When at just below room temperature, add the lemon juice, pour into a glass jar, and refrigerate for up to 6 months.

Coleslaw

This is a very simple recipe, but a real staple, and one that almost everybody likes. When I make it as a salad for friends, I never blend it into a paste. I like it best when it is chunky. However if you want to make this for the pastrami sandwich (see recipe, page 79), you can go ahead and blitz the ingredients in a food processor to create more of a spreadable paste.

Ingredients

300 g (10 ¹/₂ oz) white cabbage, shredded
50 g (1 ³/₄ oz) carrots, shredded
175 ml (5 ¹/₂ fl oz) good-quality mayonnaise
2 tablespoons white wine vinegar
¹/₂ teaspoon celery seed
1 tablespoon sugar
salt and black pepper

Method

In a large bowl, combine the cabbage and the carrots. In a small bowl, mix together the mayonnaise, vinegar, celery seed, sugar, salt and pepper. Add this dressing to the cabbage mixture, toss together, and chill for at least 30 minutes. The flavours blend better that way.

Almond, Parmesan AND Basil Pesto

Pesto has taken the world by storm over the last few decades. The classic recipe, pesto alla genovese, uses pecorino cheese and pine nuts. I prefer our creation. It's a little less oily since we use toasted almonds instead of pine nuts, and Parmesan is a bit less sharp.

Ingredients

3 garlic cloves, peeled
100 g (3 ½ oz) almonds, skinned, and roasted until golden
200 g (7 oz) fresh basil leaves
125 ml (4 fl oz) extra-virgin olive oil
80 g (2 ¾ oz) Parmesan cheese, grated
salt and black pepper

Method

In a food processor, blitz the garlic and almonds together to make a coarse paste. Add the basil, and cover with lid. While running the machine, slowly add the olive oil. You don't want to make a soup out of this, so be careful not to over-blitz. Make sure your basil maintains some of its structure. Scoop into a bowl, and stir in the Parmesan for a nice chunky pesto. Then add salt and pepper to taste. The secret of leftover pesto is that it freezes well.

Sun-Dried Tomato

AND

Green Olive Tapenade

We created this for our classic tuna sandwich. Brown sugar really grounds the intense flavours of the olives and sun-dried tomatoes. Be sure to use the best-quality olive oil you can find.

Method

Put all of the ingredients except the green olives and black pepper into the food processor, and blend until a coarse mixture is formed. Remove, and transfer to a bowl. Put the green olives into the food processor bowl, pulse until just chopped, and fold into the tomato mixture. Add pepper to taste. You can add more olive oil if you want to use this as a dip.

Ingredients

250 g (9 oz) sun-dried tomatoes packed in olive oil, drained
1 teaspoon dark brown sugar
2 garlic cloves, peeled
4 tablespoons extra-virgin olive oil
250 g (9 oz) green olives, pitted
black pepper

Wasabi Mayo

We wanted a good wasabi flavour without too powerful a kick, so we came up with this recipe. Combining with mayo tames the sharpness of the wasabi and gives it a nice creamy texture. The hint of lime balances it all out.

Ingredients

1 teaspoon wasabi paste
1 teaspoon freshly squeezed lime juice
120 ml (4 fl oz) good-quality mayonnaise

Method

Combine the ingredients well. It's better to make this mayo the day before so the flavours marry. You can also use powdered wasabi: use ½ teaspoon mixed with a little water, to make a paste. Store in the refrigerator, tightly covered with plastic wrap, until ready to serve.

Honey Mustard Sauce

We originally made this spread to go with our meatloaf sandwich (see recipe, page 80), but it also goes great with all kinds of dishes.

Ingredients

100 g (3 ½ oz) wholegrain mustard
100 ml (3 ½ fl oz) honey, the runny kind

Method

Whisk the ingredients together in a bowl and you're good to go.

We call this 'Not-Fried' Aubergine because we used to fry the aubergine. For our Hummus with Grilled Veggies and Rocket sandwich (see recipe, page 74) we changed the recipe. This way is healthier and you need far less olive oil. This recipe has its origins in the Egyptian kitchen and has always been a nice complement to our antipasti menu.

Ingredients

2 medium aubergines (eggplants), quartered
8 tablespoons olive oil

For the marinade
25 g (1 oz) fresh coriander (cilantro), stalks and leaves
1 lemon, zest only
$\frac{1}{2}$ lemon, juiced
2 garlic cloves, peeled and finely chopped
8 tablespoons olive oil
1 $\frac{1}{2}$ teaspoons ground cumin
black pepper

Method

Preheat the oven to 185°C (365°F). In a large bowl, toss the aubergine with the 8 tablespoons of olive oil. Transfer to an oven dish. Bake for 40 minutes, or until the pieces are on the crispy side. Most of us have learned to cook aubergines until golden brown. But you want to go a little further for this recipe, and cook them until they caramelise and are a very dark brown. This will keep them crispy in the marinade.

Remove from the oven and drain on paper towels. Transfer to a large bowl.

For the marinade, finely chop the stalks of the coriander and roughly chop the leaves. Add all of the ingredients together and pour over the aubergine.

Our Grilled Peppers

Peperonata *(grilled peppers) is a classic Italian antipasto. The flavours of the fire-roasted peppers, and the snap of the capers with the fresh garlic and parsley, give this dish its popularity around the world.*

Ingredients

6 peppers (capsicums) (a mixture of green, yellow and red), deseeded and cut into quarters
20 g (³/₄ oz) parsley, leaves only
2 garlic cloves, peeled
1 tablespoon capers
8 tablespoons olive oil

Method

Heat the chargrill pan or plate until very hot. Lay the peppers on the chargrill pan and cook them nicely until the edges are blackened. Chop together the parsley, garlic and capers until combined, then add the olive oil. Transfer peppers and dressing to a bowl and store in a glass jar in the fridge. When covered completely in oil, the peppers will stay delicious for weeks.

Grilled Courgettes

Grilling is always a favourite way to cook with us because it caramelises the sugars in the vegetables and brings out their natural sweetness. And they look cool with the black grill lines on them. If you are using these courgettes in a sandwich, salt and pepper them afterwards, not before. If you'd like to dress them up, just chop some fresh mint and garlic, and sprinkle over the courgettes. Courgettes and basil are also a perfect marriage, call me old-fashioned, so pesto goes perfectly.

Method

Heat the chargrill pan or plate until very hot. It's better to use a chargrill pan for these courgettes because you want the black lines on the slices, and it needs to be very hot to make sure the courgettes don't turn mushy. Arrange the courgette discs on the chargrill pan. Grill, without moving them around. Lightly season with salt and pepper before serving. If you would like to, finely chop the mint and garlic together, and scatter over the courgettes.

Ingredients

2 courgettes (zucchini), cut in 1 cm (1/2 inch) discs
olive oil
salt and black pepper

Optional
2 tablespoons fresh mint leaves
1 small garlic clove

These were designed specifically to go with our Goat's Cheese with Balsamic Onions and Rocket sandwich (see recipe, page 73), made with focaccia bread. But we also use them on our antipasti platters coupled with crumbled goat's cheese.

Method

Prepare the chargrill pan or plate until very hot, and preheat the oven to 175°C (350°F). Leave the skin and roots on the onions, and quarter them lengthways. This will stop them from falling apart when you grill them. Now remove the onion skins.

Arrange the onion pieces on the chargrill pan and grill until black lines appear, about 8 minutes. Transfer to an oven dish and pop in the oven for 25 minutes. Remove the dish from the oven, and immediately douse the onions with the vinegar and sprinkle with pepper. Leave the onions to drink up the vinegar. Any remaining liquor (it thickens nicely) is delicious drizzled over all sorts of dishes.

Ingredients

2 medium red onions, quartered
250 ml (9 fl oz) good-quality balsamic vinegar
coarsely ground black pepper

Roasted Pumpkin with Honey and Flaked Almonds

This antipasto is featured in our Roasted Pumpkin with Goat's Cheese sandwich (see recipe, page 84). We also use it in our mini-quiches and on antipasti platters.

Ingredients

500 g (1 lb 2 oz) pumpkin or butternut squash
4 tablespoons olive oil
25 g (1 oz) flaked almonds
2 tablespoons honey, the runny kind

Method

Preheat the oven to 175°C (350°F). Peel the pumpkin so that you get into the deep orange colour, and chop into 2 cm ($^3/_4$ inch) cubes. Toss well in the olive oil. Add the almonds and drizzle over the honey. Line a baking dish with baking paper and spread the pumpkin in the dish. Bake 40 minutes, or until the pumpkin is tender and the almonds are golden and crunchy.

In Australia you can get every sort of dried tomato: semi-dried, sun-dried, the whole gamut. I loved the semi-dried ones, because they had a juiciness to them and they were less chewy than the traditional sun-dried version. So when I started Small World I began the search for the perfect dried tomato for our shop. I tried leaving them in a low-heated oven overnight, and every other kind of method to get the perfect tomato. Finally, I found this technique. It's so easy and always works.

Method

Preheat the oven to 175°C (350°F). Lay the tomatoes, flat side up, in an oven dish. Drizzle, and then rub the olive oil onto the tomatoes (this will help get the seasonings to stick). Sprinkle over the other ingredients, and place the dish in the middle of the oven. Bake 60 minutes, remove from the oven, and set aside to cool. Refrigerate the tomatoes in a tightly covered dish for up to 4 days. You can chop up the tomatoes, too, to make relishes and sauces.

Ingredients

10 tomatoes, Roma (plum) or good-quality, ripe vine-tomatoes, halved
8 tablespoons extra-virgin olive oil
2 teaspoons dried thyme or dried oregano
1 teaspoon sugar (optional)
1 teaspoon sea salt
1 teaspoon coarsely ground black pepper

Roasted Chicken Thighs

In the beginning... when Small World first opened, Giovanna, a wonderful young Peruvian woman, worked with us. Her mother made food that she would sell in the market in Lima, including chicken cooked this way. She called it **pollo alla brasa.**

Ingredients

¹/₄ teaspoon mustard powder
¹/₄ teaspoon muscovado sugar
2 large garlic cloves, peeled
100 ml (3 ¹/₂ fl oz) red wine vinegar
200 ml (7 fl oz) sunflower oil
¹/₂ teaspoon coarsely ground black pepper
sea salt
500 g (1 lb 2 oz) chicken thighs, boneless and skinless

Method

Preheat the oven to 175°C (350°F). Place all the ingredients except the chicken thighs in a food processor, and blend until well mixed. Arrange the chicken thighs in an ovenproof dish, pour over the vinegar-oil mixture, and toss well.

Bake 30 minutes, and drain off and discard any liquid. Return the chicken to the oven and bake a further 15 minutes. You can check if the chicken is ready by pulling a thigh apart. It should not be pink, but white and still moist. Remove from the oven and set aside to cool.

To use in sandwiches, break up the pieces with your hands, or chop into bite-size pieces.

Roasted Turkey Breast

Turkey varies in availability from country to country. It's readily available and widely-used in the United States, while in the Netherlands it's a speciality item and only to be found in poultry shops. If you are inspired to roast your own turkey breast, here's how we roast ours.

Method

Preheat the oven to 175°C (350°F). Rinse the turkey breast in cold water and thoroughly pat dry. Heat the olive oil in a large frying pan over a high flame until it's very hot. Sprinkle the turkey breast with salt and pepper, then place in the hot pan. Be careful for splatters. Sear it for about 4 minutes on each side, or until golden brown. Wrap in two layers of kitchen foil, folding in the sides like a big envelope. Place in a baking pan and bake for 1 1/2 hours.

Remove the turkey breast from the oven and leave it in the foil to cool. For sandwiches, it's best to roast the turkey breast the day before, as it's easier to slice. Use a very sharp knife, and vary the thickness of the slices to your taste.

Ingredients

1 turkey breast (about 600 g/1 lb 5 oz)
1 tablespoon olive oil
salt and black pepper

Classic Meatloaf

This is the meatloaf we use on our Meatloaf with Honey Mustard Sauce sandwich (see recipe, page 80). It also works great as a main course. For a stylish presentation, wrap the bacon around the outside of the meatloaf, instead of frying it up and adding it to the mix. Meatloaf is the ultimate feelgood meal on a cold winter's day. This recipe makes a large meatloaf, good for about 10 sandwiches, so you can freeze the portions you don't use.

Ingredients

¹/₄ loaf day-old crusty bread such as ciabatta
85 g (3 oz) bacon, cut into 5 mm (¹/₄ inch) cubes
2 medium white onions, finely chopped
6 tablespoons roughly chopped parsley
1.25 kg (2 lb 12 oz) minced meat, ¹/₂ beef, ¹/₂ pork
2 eggs
4 tablespoons wholegrain mustard
4 tablespoons Worcestershire Sauce
12 tablespoons ketchup (tomato sauce)
sea salt
1 teaspoon freshly ground black pepper
2 tablespoons olive oil
1 ¹/₂ teaspoons granulated onion

Method

Preheat the oven the 175°C (350°F). Toast the bread until dry and crumbly enough to turn into a powder. We blitz it in a mixer, but it can be done by hand. If you use your hand, make sure the crumbs are powdery or you'll get a chewy meatloaf. Crisp the bacon in a frying pan until well-browned and crunchy. Use a spoon to transfer to a large mixing bowl, and leave the fat in the pan. Add the onions to the pan and sauté over medium heat until translucent. Add the parsley, and sweat it over low heat for a couple of minutes. Transfer to the bowl and add the meat, eggs, mustard, Worcestershire Sauce, half the ketchup, and salt and pepper. With your hands, fold everything together really well but without over-kneading it.

Transfer the mixture to a clean work surface and shape into an oval loaf about 30 cm (12 inches) long. Don't press down on it–you want to keep it in log form. In a small saucepan, heat the olive oil, remaining ketchup and the granulated onion over low heat. Using a large spoon, glaze the meatloaf with this sauce and transfer to the oven. Bake for 1 hour. Remove from oven and set aside to cool.

For sandwiches, it's best to make the meatloaf well-ahead, as it's easier to cut into clean slices when cold.

Sandwiches

At Small World we like to make generously filled sandwiches. These recipes are based on that preference, but it's easy to adapt each one to your own taste. Use the best ingredients you can find: it really makes all the difference!

A Word on Making Sandwiches

*Always use a sharp knife to slice the
bread and cut the sandwiches.
When a certain type of bread is the best to use, it is
mentioned in the recipe, but most sandwiches can be made
with all sorts of bread. Here also goes that quality makes
all the difference, so buy the best bread you can get.*

*Tomatoes should be ripe and thinly sliced, and
arranged in layers on the sandwich.
Himalayan pink salt is our favourite seasoning.*

*All recipes serve 2, so the ingredients are based on
2 sandwiches. The method in each recipe describes
how to make 1 sandwich.
Cut each sandwich in half with a sharp knife when ready.
It looks nicer and is easier to eat.*

Prosciutto with Marinated Artichoke Hearts, Lemon Olive Oil and Rocket

This is an all-time favourite that we've had on the menu since the beginning. I love artichoke hearts, and they pair really well with a sweet prosciutto ham. Make sure you use good-quality artichoke hearts that are marinated in oil, not the tinned ones in vinegar. Those are just wrong.

Ingredients

a drizzle Lemon Olive Oil (see recipe, page 14)
120 g (4 ¼ oz) prosciutto (Parma ham), thinly sliced
150 g (5 ½ oz) Italian marinated artichoke hearts
salt and black pepper
a handful young rocket (arugula) leaves

Method

Slice a focaccia in half evenly and drizzle both sides generously with the lemon olive oil. With your hand, tear the prosciutto into a few pieces. Scrunch these 'ribbons' over one side of the sandwich, then evenly distribute the artichoke hearts over them. Black pepper and artichokes go great together, so be generous with the pepper mill. Scatter the rocket leaves on top. Don't press down on the sandwich when putting it together as these ingredients are easily flattened, so be careful.

This is a classic American BLT. We just added avocado to give it an Australian slant. The combination of smooth creamy avocado and crispy bacon, especially when it's still warm, is a winning team. This one is great on a crunchy ciabatta.

Avocado, Bacon, Tomato AND Mayo

Method

In a pan, crisp up the bacon and drain on any extra egg cartons you have around (it's a great trick). Slice a ciabatta in half and spread one side generously with the mayo. Slice the avocado over the other half of the bread, don't mash it. I find that slices look more stylish and have a bit more bite. Squeeze over a little lemon juice, and salt and pepper well. Layer the crispy bacon over the avocado followed by the tomato slices, and give another grind of salt and pepper. Scrunch the lettuce leaves in your hand and place them on top. Cover with the other slice of ciabatta.

Ingredients

100 g (3 ½ oz) bacon (*katenspek*) or pancetta
4 tablespoons good-quality mayonnaise
1 large Hass avocado
½ lemon
salt and black pepper
1 large, ripe Roma (plum) tomato, cut into 6 slices
4 crispy iceberg lettuce leaves

Having had the good fortune to have lived in Italy and worked in some fine Italian restaurants, I know that beef carpaccio is a classic standard that everyone loves. I really wanted it on my menu, so I turned it into a sandwich. You can use Parmigiano Reggiano or Grana Padano cheese depending on your budget. This is best on a focaccia, but works well on a crunchy ciabatta also.

Carpaccio with Sun-Dried Tomatoes and Parmesan Shavings

Method

Cut the bread in half and drizzle both sides with the lemon olive oil. Layer the carpaccio on one slice of the bread, squeeze over a few drops of lemon juice, and season with salt and pepper. Now layer on the Parmesan shavings, scatter over the sun-dried tomatoes, then the rocket leaves. Cover with the second slice of bread.

Ingredients

a drizzle Lemon Olive Oil (see recipe, page 14)
100 g (3 $\frac{1}{2}$ oz) good-quality beef carpaccio
(if possible, from your local butcher)
$\frac{1}{2}$ lemon
salt and black pepper
50 g (1 $\frac{3}{4}$ oz) Parmesan cheese, in one piece,
and shaved
40 g (1 $\frac{1}{2}$ oz) sun-dried tomatoes packed in olive
oil, drained, and cut into 1 cm ($\frac{1}{2}$ inch) pieces
1 handful young rocket (arugula) leaves

Roasted Turkey Breast with Crispy Bacon and Tomato

This is our answer to the classic club sandwich. We wanted a more rustic version. So we skipped the supermarket white-bread slices and went for the focaccia. It also tastes good on a crunchy brown bread.

Ingredients

100 g (3 ½ oz) bacon
3 tablespoons good-quality mayonnaise
2 tablespoons wholegrain dijon mustard
200 g (7 oz) Roasted Turkey Breast (see recipe,
page 39), cut in thin slices
1 large, ripe Roma (plum) tomato, cut into 6 slices
salt and black pepper
2 handfuls baby-leaf lettuce

Method

In a pan, crisp up the bacon, and drain on egg cartons if you have any lying around (or use paper towels). Cut the bread in half and spread the mayo on one side, the mustard on the other. Layer the roasted turkey breast slices on top of the mayo. Place the tomato slices on top of the turkey breast, and season with salt and pepper. Layer over the bacon, and scatter with the baby-leaf lettuce. Cover with the mustard-coated slice of bread.

Roasted Chicken with Avocado, Mayo and Red Onion

This sandwich was inspired by one I used to eat at a local deli here in Amsterdam. Although the combination is similar, it took me a while to figure out what made it so special. It was the combination of onion with avocado. The deli used minced white onion. When I opened Small World I wanted to make a more robust version of the sandwich. Chunks of roasted chicken from a common South American recipe (pollo alla brasa) combined with red onion slices, avocado and a seasoning of lemon juice, salt and pepper, give this sandwich the 'salsa effect' that gives it its special edge.

Ingredients

3 tablespoons good-quality mayonnaise
250 g (9 oz) Roasted Chicken Thighs (see recipe, page 38), in chunks
1 large Hass avocado
1/2 lemon
salt and black pepper
1 small red onion, very thinly sliced
2 handfuls baby-leaf lettuce, the crunchier the better

Method

Slice the bread in half and spread one side with the mayo. Place the roasted chicken on top. Slice the avocado onto the other side of the bread, press down firmly, squeeze over a few drops of lemon juice, and salt and pepper it well. Break up the red onion rings and scatter them over the chicken. Top it off with the baby-leaf lettuce, cover with the other side of the bread.

Fresh Sashimi Tuna with Sun-Dried Tomato and Green Olive Tapenade

This sandwich isn't really inspired by any other filling combinations I've seen on my travels. I just wanted to have 'sashimi' tuna on a sandwich. It's fantastic on focaccia. Originally I thought about a ginger tapenade, but later changed it to this Mediterranean version that has become a staple in the shop. What's great about tapenade is that you can make lots of it and serve it as a dip, or on other sandwiches.

Ingredients

4 tablespoons Sun-Dried Tomato and Green
Olive Tapenade (see recipe, page 19)
200 g (7 oz) sashimi-grade tuna, in one piece
as required olive oil
salt and black pepper
$^1/_2$ lemon
1 handful young rocket (arugula) leaves
to taste Lemon Olive Oil (see recipe, page 14)

Method

Heat a chargrill pan or plate on high. While the pan is heating, slice open the focaccia and spread one side generously with the tapenade. Coat your chunk of fresh tuna in olive oil, and rub some of the oil in so that it's not dripping. Salt and pepper this now. Sear the tuna on each side for no more than a minute or two, depending on the thickness of the steak. Make sure you don't cook it through; you want to keep that delicate sashimi-raw centre.

Take the tuna out of the pan, and let it sit for a minute so that it doesn't flake when you cut it. At the shop we have a professional slicer but, at home, you'll have to mimic this with the thinnest, sharpest knife you've got. Slice the tuna steak in 5 mm ($^1/_4$ inch) thick pieces and layer these on top of the tapenade. Give it a squeeze of lemon and some salt and pepper before piling on the rocket. Drizzle the lemon olive oil on the other slice of bread, then place on top to make the sandwich.

Special Tuna with Avocado, Wasabi Mayo AND Rocket

After offering the Fresh Sashimi Tuna with Sun-Dried Tomato and Green Olive Tapenade sandwich (see recipe, page 59) in the shop for 10 years, one day we decided to make a summer version. This has now taken over as the most popular sandwich. I still love the other version, which I find more of a winter choice. I prefer it on ciabatta or a crunchy white bread.

Method

Heat a chargrill pan or plate on high. While the pan is heating, slice the ciabatta open and spread one side with the wasabi mayo and some rocket leaves. Coat your chunk of fresh tuna in olive oil, and rub some of the oil in so that it's not dripping. Salt and pepper this now. Sear the tuna on each side for no more than a minute or two, depending on the thickness of the steak. Make sure you don't cook it through; you want to keep that delicate sashimi-raw centre.

Take the tuna out of the pan, and let it sit for a minute so that it doesn't flake when you cut it. At the shop we have a professional slicer but, at home, you'll have to mimic this with the thinnest, sharpest knife you've got. Slice the tuna in 5 mm (¼ inch) pieces and layer on top of the mayo and rocket. Give it a squeeze of lemon and salt and pepper, then place the coriander on top. Slice the avocado onto the other side of bread and press firmly. Place on top to make the sandwich.

Ingredients

3 tablespoons Wasabi Mayo (see recipe, page 20)
1 handful young rocket (arugula) leaves
200 g (7 oz) sashimi-grade tuna
as required olive oil
salt and black pepper
½ lemon
a few sprigs fresh coriander (cilantro)
1 large Hass avocado

Chicken, Pesto WITH Grilled AND Marinated Veggies

This is one in a series of our pesto sandwiches with grilled vegetables. Pesto is always delicious and there's always a good excuse to use it. This sandwich combines our oven-roasted chicken with a trio of marinated vegetables–tomatoes, courgettes and aubergines–each prepared in a different fashion. This filling also works well on focaccia or ciabatta.

Method

Slice the bread and spread the mayo on one half. Place the chicken pieces on top of the mayo, which will prevent them from sliding out of the sandwich. Arrange the grilled and marinated vegetables alternately over the chicken, season with salt and pepper, and top with the baby-leaf lettuce. Spread the pesto on the other half of the bread, and place on top.

Ingredients

3 tablespoons good-quality mayonnaise
250 g (9 oz) Roasted Chicken Thighs (see recipe, page 38), in pieces
200 g (7 oz) mixed grilled and marinated vegetables (see recipes, pages 22, 28 and 36)
4 tablespoons Pesto (see recipe, page 18)
2 handfuls baby-leaf lettuce
salt and black pepper

Tuna Salad with Fresh Coriander, Lime, Avocado and Red Onion

There are so many varieties of tuna salad that it makes the choice of which one to serve a difficult one. I love it with chunks of green apple, parsley, green olives and lemon. The Small World tuna salad has a South American zest that we couldn't resist. This sandwich filling works on any good bread.

Ingredients

320 g (11 ¼ oz) tinned tuna, drained
2 small stalks celery, cut in 5 mm (¼ inch) pieces
1 small red onion, finely chopped
15 g (½ oz) fresh coriander (cilantro)
½ teaspoon very finely grated lime zest
4 tablespoons good-quality mayonnaise
1 large tomato, sliced
2 handfuls crunchy romaine (cos) lettuce
salt and black pepper
1 large Hass avocado, sliced
½ lime
a dash Tabasco sauce

Method

To make the tuna salad, mix the tuna, celery, red onion, leaves and stems of the coriander and the lime zest in a bowl. Gently fold these ingredients together, then incorporate 2 tablespoons of the mayo into the mixture. Make sure you leave some nice hearty chunks of fish intact, as you don't want it to become a paste.

Cut the bread in half, and spread each piece with 1 tablespoon of mayo. Layer the tuna salad on one piece of bread, top with the tomato slices, season with a turn of salt and pepper, and cover with the lettuce. Arrange the avocado slices on the other piece of the bread and gently press down, into the bread. Drizzle with lime juice, and lightly season with salt and pepper. Place the two sides together and serve sliced in half. A dash of Tabasco nicely spices up this combination.

Avocado with Wasabi Mayo, Grilled Veggies and Red Onion

This sandwich was created by Jan, who used ingredients that we had available to make her own signature sandwich. It became a big hit. We needed a California-style veggie sandwich and this fitted the bill. We use four vegetable sorts: roasted tomatoes, grilled courgettes, fire-roasted peppers and oven-baked aubergines. And what goes better with 'California-style' than a wrap? It's also great with wholegrain bread or focaccia.

Ingredients

3 tablespoons Wasabi Mayo (see recipe, page 20)
200 g (7 oz) mixed grilled and marinated vegetables (see recipes, pages 22, 26, 28 and 36)
salt and black pepper
1 small red onion, thinly sliced
2 handfuls young rocket (arugula) leaves and baby-leaf lettuce, combined
1 large Hass avocado, sliced
$^1/_2$ lemon

Method

Slice the bread in half. Spread the wasabi mayo on one half of the bread. Arrange the grilled vegetables on top, and give it all a turn of salt and pepper. Spread over the red onion slices, and top with the baby-leaf lettuce and rocket leaves. Arrange the avocado slices on the other side of the bread and gently press down, into the bread. Sprinkle with a squeeze of lemon and some salt and pepper, and close the sandwich.

For a wrap, spread the wasabi mayo over the whole wrap to the edges. Make a 4 cm (1 $^1/_2$ inch) wide strip of avocado slices in the centre of the wrap, leaving about 2 cm ($^3/_4$ inch) on either side. Lemon, salt and pepper this. Layer the vegetables above (not on top of) the avocado slices. Add your red onions, top it all with baby-leaf lettuce and rocket leaves, and then you're ready to wrap it. This can be difficult, but I find the best way is to roll it half way, then fold in the sides and finish rolling it. If you need to, add a dab of wasabi mayo to the last bit to make it stick.

If you want to impress, put it on a chargrill pan or plate for a couple of minutes until you get some grill lines.

This is a summer version of our sandwich, Pesto Melt with Taleggio and Grilled Veggies (see recipe, page 92) and it reminds me of when I was a kid in Australia. I used to go to the beach and there were surf shacks that served smoothies and these kinds of veggie sandwiches. I always loved them. Pesto had already become such a staple that it was no longer just Italian, it was used in all kinds of bohemian dishes. Here, creamy, mild ricotta plays off the robust and aromatic flavours of the pesto. This is also great on focaccia, or follow the steps for making it as a wrap in our Avocado with Wasabi Mayo, Grilled Veggies and Red Onion (see recipe, page 69).

Ricotta with Pesto, Lettuce and Grilled Veggies

Ingredients

6 tablespoons ricotta, preferably sheep-milk
200 g (7 oz) mixed grilled and marinated vegetables (see recipes, pages 22, 26, 28 and 36)
4 tablespoons Pesto (see recipe, page 18)
2 handfuls baby-leaf lettuce
salt and black pepper

Method

Slice your bread in half. Spread the ricotta on one half with the veggies on top, arranging them in alternate layers. Season with salt and pepper to taste, and top with lettuce. Spread the pesto on the other piece of bread, and put both halves together.

Goat's Cheese with Balsamic Onions and Rocket

We use goat's cheese a lot in *Small World*. *This combination of contrasting flavours–the sharpness of the onion, the tangy sweetness of the balsamic vinegar and the mild creaminess of the soft goat's cheese–creates a taste sensation.* Great on a crusty ciabatta or crunchy brown bread.

Ingredients

150 g (5 ½ oz) soft goat's cheese, such as a
French chèvre
150 g (5 ½ oz) Balsamic Onions (see recipe,
page 31), chopped in large pieces
a handful young rocket (arugula) leaves
black pepper

Method

Cut the bread in half, and slather the goat's cheese evenly over both slices. Layer the balsamic onion pieces on top of one side of the bread. Give it all a good grind of pepper, top with rocket leaves, and put both bread halves together.

I grew up in Melbourne where there's a huge Lebanese population and, of course, Lebanese food. I've always loved hummus and I used it when I had to make a sandwich for the shop. It's totally vegan and really tasty. The classic Middle Eastern version is puréed and creamy, but I decided to give it a rougher texture with a bit of bite by adding fresh coriander. It's much better if you steer clear of tinned chickpeas as the brine makes them soggy. In the shop we make this sandwich with courgettes, oven-roasted tomatoes and aubergines, but it's amazing with just the Small World 'Not-Fried' Aubergine (see recipe, page 22) antipasto.

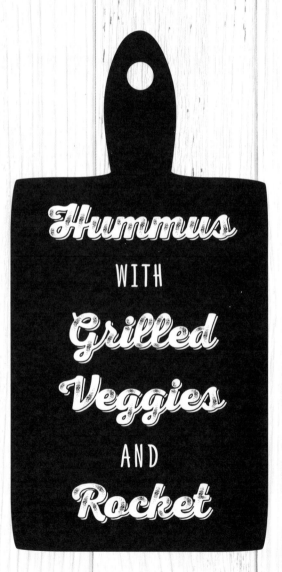

Hummus WITH Grilled Veggies AND Rocket

Ingredients

300 g (10 ½ oz) Coriander Hummus
(see recipe, page 12)
½ lemon
salt and black pepper
200 g (7 oz) mixed grilled and marinated
vegetables (see recipes, pages 22, 28 and 36)
a handful rocket (arugula) leaves

Method

Cut the bread in half and spread 2 tablespoons of the hummus on each piece. Give it all a nice squeeze of lemon and add some salt and pepper. Arrange the grilled and marinated vegetables in alternate layers over the hummus on one side of bread, the rocket on top. Cover with the other side of the bread to make the sandwich.

Warm Pastrami WITH Coleslaw, Emmental Cheese AND Mustard

This is a variation of a classic NYC favourite. My American friends insisted that this should be on Small World's menu, so we devised a special version of our own. The texture and saltiness of the pastrami and the sweetness of emmental complement each other, while the coleslaw gives the combination crunch and the wholegrain mustard a nice sharp edge. The New York classic is always on rye bread and it is really the best option.

Ingredients

300 g (10 ½ oz) pastrami (pickled beef, American-style)
6 tablespoons Coleslaw (see recipe, page 15)
2 tablespoons wholegrain mustard
120 g (4 ¼ oz) Emmental or Swiss cheese, sliced
black pepper

Method

Preheat the oven to 175°C (350°F). Sprinkle the pastrami with a little water and wrap tightly in kitchen foil. Steam in the oven for 15 minutes. Remove the pastrami from the oven and don't unwrap it yet. Cut the bread in half. Spread one slice of bread with the coleslaw, the other slice with the mustard. Lay the cheese slices on both sides of the bread, and season with pepper. Unwrap the hot pastrami and put it directly on top of the cheese. Close the sandwich as quickly as possible to keep the heat in, so the cheese gets nice and melty. Great with a cold beer.

When I was a child, my mother would often make us meatloaf for dinner. The next day we would take the leftovers to school on white bread sandwiches with tomato sauce (actually ketchup, but we call it tomato sauce). This was an Australian staple. I first started serving meatloaf at Small World as a main dish wrapped in bacon. When we turned it into a sandwich we fried up the bacon and mixed it into the meatloaf. I could hardly serve it in the shop on white bread with tomato sauce, so we came up with a more gourmet recipe. We serve it on crunchy ciabatta with Honey Mustard Sauce (see recipe, page 21).

Meatloaf with Honey Mustard Sauce

Method

Preheat the oven to 175°C (350°F). Heat the meatloaf slices in the oven for 10 minutes. Slice the bread in half and spread both sides with the honey mustard. Pile the lettuce, then the tomato slices, on one half, and season with some salt and black pepper. Arrange two slices of the warm meatloaf on top. Close the sandwich and serve immediately.

Ingredients

240 g (8 ½ oz) Classic Meatloaf (see recipe, page 41), cut into 1 cm (½ inch) thick slices
4 tablespoons Honey Mustard Sauce (see recipe, page 21)
2 handfuls baby-leaf lettuce
1 large tomato, sliced
salt and black pepper

Spicy Salami with Grilled Courgettes and Taleggio

This sandwich was inspired by a pasta sauce that I used to make at Toscanini, a great restaurant here in Amsterdam where I once worked. The combination of flavours and textures impressed me. I always think of it as Small World's upgrade of the pepperoni pizza. Make sure you get a nice and spicy Italian salami–the Sicilian variety with chilli peppers is perfect.

Ingredients

a splash Lemon Olive Oil (see recipe, page 14)
200 g (7 oz) spicy salami, sliced
160 g (5 ¹/₂ oz) Grilled Courgettes (see recipe, page 28)
100 g (3 ¹/₂ oz) Taleggio cheese
coarsely ground black pepper
a good handful rocket (arugula)

Method

Preheat the oven to 175°C (350°F). Cut the bread in half and generously drizzle each side with the lemon olive oil. Tear the spicy salami slices into large pieces, to give them more volume, and arrange on both slices of the bread. Chop the courgette discs into bite-size pieces, and strew them evenly over both sides of the sandwich. Cut the cheese into 2 cm (³/₄ inch) squares. This cheese can be tricky to cut since it's so creamy, so use a hot knife if you need to. Arrange the pieces over both sides of the bread and place, open-face, on an oven tray.

Heat the sandwich in the oven until the cheese is melted and the salami has given off its oil, approximately 8 minutes. Just when it's out of the oven and still hot, give it a good dose of pepper. Scatter over the rocket and put the two sides together.

This was made by Zoe, one of my favourite people who ever worked in Small World. She made a lot of the cookies and cakes we serve, and she invented this sandwich. For some reason girls love it, so I teasingly call it 'the girl's sandwich', though guys order it too. But they like it made with bacon, to make it more of a 'manwich'. Heavenly on a crunchy piece of bread.

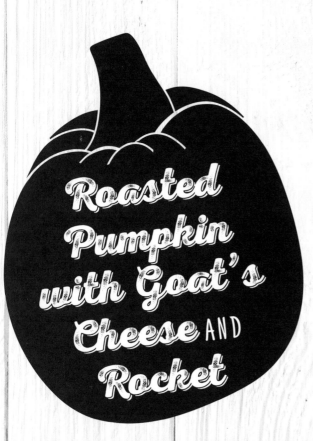

Roasted Pumpkin with Goat's Cheese AND Rocket

Method

Preheat the oven to 175°C (350°F). Slice the bread in two, and slather the goat's cheese on both sides. Place an even layer of pumpkin on one of the sides, give a twirl of pepper, and put both slices of bread into the oven for 4 minutes. Scatter the rocket over the melted goat's cheese, and serve while warm.

Ingredients

150 g (5 ½ oz) soft goat's cheese, such as
French chèvre
150g (5 ½ oz) Roasted Pumpkin (see recipe,
page 32)
black pepper
a handful rocket (arugula)

Turkey Melt with Roasted Peppers and Swiss Cheese

This is Ray's sandwich. He was the chef at Small World for 12 years and created a lot of our dishes. This is one of his finest. The sweet, smoky taste of the roast peppers is a nice contrast with the salty cheese and, when it's all melted together, it's divine. Then along came Clarence, who elaborated on the sandwich by adding salami and Tabasco, and making it with crusty ciabatta. Thus its name, The Clarence. It's a huge hit with the locals.

Method

Preheat the oven to 175°C (350°F). Slice the bread in half, and treat it like an open-face sandwich. Spread both slices of bread with mayo, then a layer of sliced turkey breast, followed by the roasted peppers. Place a slice of cheese on each side, and season with pepper. Put into the oven for 4 minutes, or until the cheese is nicely melted. Throw on the rocket, and serve while still warm.

Ingredients

6 tablespoons good-quality mayonnaise
300 g (10 ½ oz) Roasted Turkey Breast (see recipe, page 39), cut into very thin slices
200 g (7 oz) Grilled Peppers (see recipe, page 26), cut into 2x2 cm (¾ inch) chunks
120 g (4 ¼ oz) Swiss cheese or Emmental, sliced
freshly ground black pepper
a handful rocket (arugula)

Tuna Melt with Fresh Coriander and Swiss Cheese

Who doesn't love a tuna melt? We added a twist to this sandwich by using our own tuna salad, which features fresh coriander in the mix. The first time I heard about tuna melts was when I worked at the Egg Cream here, in Amsterdam, years ago, and I used to make them in a pan, melted in butter. Rather than give anyone a coronary, we melt ours in the oven. This one is also really good with Tabasco.

Ingredients

4 tablespoons good-quality mayonnaise
350 g (12 oz) Tuna Salad (see recipe, page 66)
1 large, ripe Roma (plum) tomato, cut into 6 slices
salt
120 g (4 ¼ oz) Swiss cheese or Emmental, sliced
a few leaves romaine (cos) lettuce

Method

Preheat the oven to 175°C (350°F). Slice a ciabatta in half. Spread each slice with mayo, then with the tuna salad. Place 3 slices of tomato on one side, and give it some salt. Place a slice of cheese on each side. Put in the oven for 4 minutes, or until the cheese has melted. Once out of the oven, rip some of the lettuce leaves on top, close the sandwich, and serve.

Thai-Style Fish Cakes with Avocado and Wasabi Mayo

*I really think that this is such an original sandwich. It kind of evolved out of the food we were already serving in the shop. The fish cakes alone were already a big hit.
Try them with ciabatta or crunchy brown bread!*

Ingredients

2 Thai-Style Fish Cakes (see recipe, page 125)
1 large Hass avocado
$1/2$ lemon
salt and black pepper
1 small red onion, very thinly sliced
3 tablespoons Wasabi Mayo (see recipe, page 20)
a few leaves romaine (cos) lettuce
2 tablespoons Thai Sweet Chilli Sauce

Method

If you've frozen the fish cakes ahead of time, defrost them. Preheat the oven to 175°C (350°F). Cut the fish cakes in half, arrange on a tray, and heat in the oven for 5 minutes.

Cut the bread in half, and arrange the slices of $1/2$ avocado over one piece. Squeeze over some lemon juice, and give a good grind of salt and pepper. Top this with the slices of red onion. On the other half, spread a tablespoon of the wasabi mayo, and top this with some crunchy lettuce. Remove the fish cakes from the oven. Place two half-cakes across the avocado side of the sandwich, and drizzle over some chilli sauce. Put both halves together. Great with a nice cold Singha beer.

Pesto Melt with Taleggio AND Grilled Veggies

I like this one on a focaccia. This is the winter cousin to the Ricotta with Pesto, Lettuce and Grilled Veggies sandwich (see recipe, page 70). The melted Taleggio combines with the pesto in the oven to create a rich, sublime flavour that warms up any cold winter day in Amsterdam.

Method

Preheat the oven to 175°C (350°F). Slice the focaccia, and spread the pesto over both slices. Place the grilled and marinated vegetables evenly on one side, alternating them so that each bite is different. Dot the cheese on both sides of the bread, pepper it, and place in the oven for 5 minutes. When ready, top one side of the bread with rocket, and put it together. You'll need a napkin or two for this one!

Ingredients

6 tablespoons Pesto (see recipe, page 18)
200 g (7 oz) mixed grilled and marinated vegetables (see recipes, pages 22, 26, 28 and 36)
100 g (3 ½ oz) Taleggio cheese, cut into 2 cm (¾ inch) squares
black pepper
a handful rocket (arugula)

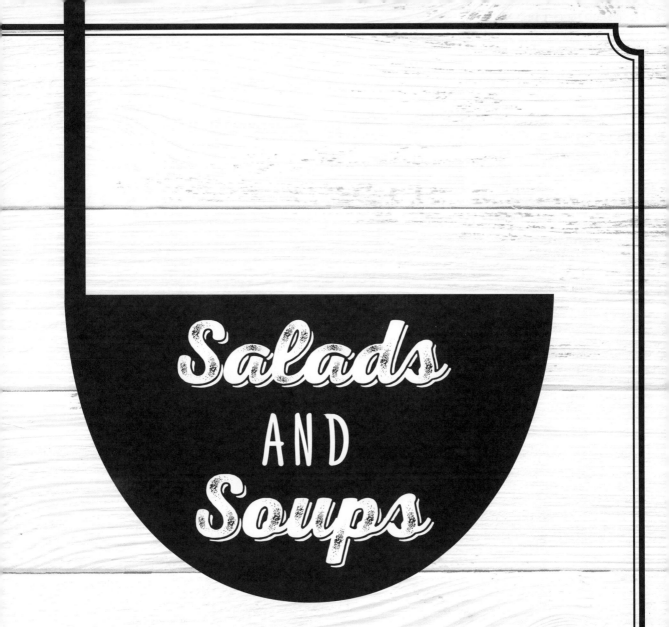

Salads AND Soups

The recipes for the salads all give small portions as side dishes. You can easily turn these into mains by tweaking the quantities, and perhaps by adding meat or fish.

All salad recipes make 4 sides.

All soup recipes serve 4.

Haricots Verts with Roasted Walnuts and Parmesan Shavings

This salad has been in Small World from Day One, and always sells out. Of all of our dishes, besides our desserts, this is the only dish that has stayed with us every day. It's still winning everyone over. Simple, but simplicity at its best.

Ingredients

75 g (2 ½ oz) walnuts
sea salt
300 g (10 ½ oz) green beans (haricots verts), topped and tailed
1 tablespoon olive oil
a few grinds black pepper
1 tablespoon dijon mustard
75 g (2 ½ oz) Parmesan cheese

Method

Preheat the oven to 175°C (350°F). Spread the walnuts over a baking tray and pop them into the oven for 10 minutes. You want them nicely roasted, and crunchy. Leave them to cool.

Bring a large saucepan of water to a boil, and lightly salt it. Add the beans to the pan and cook 3 minutes, or until al dente. Drain in a colander, and briefly rinse under cold water (this stops the cooking process). Dry the beans with a tea or dish towel and place in a large bowl. Drizzle over the olive oil and lightly toss the beans. Salt and pepper the salad now. Dot the mustard over the beans in little bits, so it mixes evenly with the beans. Break the nuts into 1 cm (½ inch) pieces, and lightly mix into the salad.

I like to use a potato peeler to shave the Parmesan into the salad, others like to grate it in. Make sure there are large strips as these look nice, and give a good bite of Parmesan. You don't want to mix the salad so much now as you need to avoid breaking the cheese into little pieces. It's now ready! Serve as a side dish with a main meal, or on a salad platter, for lunch.

Beetroot is very popular in Australia. We use it in everything, from dips to salads and burgers. We love its sweet, earthy taste. It seemed to have lost popularity in Holland, but we notice that it's definitely a hit in our shop all year around. It's great in the summer, but makes a good winter salad, too. Add a soft goat's cheese or a blue cheese to make this salad more of a main meal.

Beetroot and Apple Salad in a Toasted Cumin and Orange Dressing

Method

Place the beetroot in a bowl. Quarter and core the apples. You can choose to peel or not: some people love the apple skin, others really don't like it. Slice the apples into 2.5 mm (1/8 inch) slices and add to the beetroot, then add the onion. Stir in the cumin seeds and the zest and juice of the orange.

In a small bowl, combine the honey and vinegar, then add the sunflower oil. Pour this over the beetroot mixture and combine well. Season with salt and pepper, to taste. It's ready to eat! If you're adding cheese, then crumble it on top of the salad, but don't mix in or it will turn pink.

Ingredients

500 g (1 lb 2 oz) beetroot (beets), peeled, boiled, and cut into 2.5 mm (1/8 inch) rounds
2 apples, your favourite variety
1 small white onion, thinly sliced
2 teaspoons whole cumin seeds, lightly toasted in a dry pan
1 orange, zest and juice
1 tablespoon honey, the runny sort
75 ml (2 1/2 fl oz) white wine vinegar
125 ml (4 fl oz) sunflower oil
salt and coarsely ground black pepper

Mediterranean Couscous Salad with Fresh Herbs

Instead of a pasta salad we wanted to have something a bit more exotic. This salad is more work, but it is well worth the effort. The flavours of cumin and lemon, combined with the fresh herbs and the toasted couscous, are satisfying and delicious. It is a versatile dish that can accompany a chicken fillet, or it can be a great dish on its own. You can also add pomegranate seeds or feta cheese if you wish.

Ingredients

1 small white onion, chopped into 1 cm
(¹/₂ inch) pieces
200 ml (7 fl oz) red wine vinegar
4 tablespoons olive oil
200 g (7 oz) couscous
1 vegetable stock cube
400 ml (14 fl oz) boiling water
1 red pepper (capsicum), chopped into 1 cm
(¹/₂ inch) pieces
1 ¹/₂ teaspoons ground cumin
1 medium cucumber, peeled, but leave some
strips of skin (it's easiest to do this
with a potato peeler)
a few sprigs fresh chives
a few sprigs parsley
a few sprigs fresh coriander (cilantro)
10 fresh mint leaves
10 black olives, pitted (Kalamatas are good)
1 lemon, zest only
50 g (1 ³/₄ oz) sun-dried tomatoes packed in olive
oil, drained, and cut into strips
salt and coarsely ground black pepper

Method

Combine the onion and vinegar in a small glass bowl and set aside to marinate. Heat half the olive oil in a large frying pan or skillet over medium heat. Add the couscous and cook, stirring occasionally, for 10 minutes, or until golden brown and crisp. Dissolve the stock cube in the boiling water, pour over the couscous and remove the pan from the heat. Cover with a tea or dish towel, and as tightly as possible with a lid, to seal in the steam. Set aside to let the couscous absorb the liquid.

In another frying pan heat the remaining olive oil and sauté the pepper and cumin until the pepper is lightly cooked but not limp, about 5 minutes. Slice the cucumber lengthways in half, scoop out and discard the seeds, then slice lengthways in half again. Chop into 1 cm (¹/₂ inch) pieces. Roughly chop together the chives, parsley, fresh coriander and mint leaves. Crush the olives into bite-sized pieces with your fingers.

Transfer the couscous to a large bowl and separate the grains with a fork. Make sure there are no clumps. Now add all the ingredients, including the lemon zest and sun-dried tomatoes, season to taste, and mix well.

Spicy Broccoli and Pumpkin Salad

Salads are not just for summer. Flavourful and sweet, Spicy Broccoli and Pumpkin Salad is a great winter salad that works well as a side dish for main meals, but is also a satisfying lunch unto itself.

Ingredients

500 g (1 lb 2 oz) pumpkin or butternut squash, peeled, and cut into 1 cm (½ inch) cubes
4 tablespoons sunflower oil
1 teaspoon powdered ginger
1 teaspoon coconut sugar or raw cane sugar
½ chilli pepper, deseeded and finely chopped
sea salt and coarsely ground black pepper
500 g (1 lb 2 oz) broccoli florets
125 g (4 ½ oz) French shallots, finely sliced

Dressing
4 tablespoons rice wine vinegar
4 tablespoons sunflower oil
½ chilli pepper, deseeded, and finely chopped
3 tablespoons ginger syrup, or runny honey

Method

Preheat the oven to 175°C (350°F). Place the pumpkin in an oven dish and toss with the sunflower oil, powdered ginger, coconut sugar, chilli, salt and pepper. Place in the oven for 25 minutes, or until the pumpkin is soft but not mushy. Remove from the oven, and let cool.

Lightly boil the broccoli until al dente (about 3 minutes), strain, and transfer to a paper towel to dry. Set aside to cool.

In a salad bowl, thoroughly whisk together all the ingredients for the dressing. Add the roasted pumpkin, broccoli and shallots, and toss well.

Roasted Fennel, Feta AND Kalamata Salad

In this simple salad, the salty olives are well set-off by the sweetness of the roasted fennel, and the garlic and parsley give it all an extra kick.

Ingredients

4 fennel bulbs, rinsed well in cold water, and thinly sliced
1 garlic clove, finely chopped
3 tablespoons olive oil
salt and black pepper
100 g (3 ½ oz) Kalamata olives
3 tablespoons parsley
100 g (3 ½ oz) feta cheese

Method

Preheat the oven to 175°C (350°F). Line a baking tray with baking paper and spread over the sliced fennel. Sprinkle evenly with garlic, drizzle with olive oil, and season with salt and pepper. Transfer to the oven and bake 30 minutes; give the tray a shake halfway through the cooking time. Set aside for 10 minutes, to cool.

Meanwhile, chop the olives and parsley and crumble the feta. In a bowl, gently mix together all the ingredients, and you are ready to serve.

This is on our menu regularly as its ranking is high on my list of 'best ever' soup recipes! Try it: it is satisfying and delicious, and hits every button! Hearty, sweet, woody and with a little bite too.

Spicy Coconut and Parsnip Soup

Ingredients

6 medium parsnips, peeled, and chopped into
2 cm (¾ inch) pieces
4 tablespoons olive oil
2 teaspoons powdered ginger
2 teaspoons ground cumin
salt and black pepper
1 large white onion, chopped
2 garlic cloves, finely chopped
1 chilli pepper, deseeded (unless you
want an extra kick!)
1 litre (35 fl oz) water
1 vegetable stock cube (or chicken stock cube,
if you prefer)
500 ml (17 fl oz) coconut milk
a few sprigs fresh coriander (cilantro), leaves only

Method

Preheat the oven to 175°C (350°F). Toss the parsnips in 2 tablespoons of the olive oil, and sprinkle with the ginger, cumin, salt and pepper. Pop the dish into the oven for 25 minutes.

Add the remaining 2 tablespoons olive oil to a frying pan, and sauté the onion, garlic and chilli until the onion is translucent.

Combine the onion mixture and the parsnips in a heavy saucepan set over medium heat. Toss together for 2 minutes. Add the water and stock cube, stir together, and heat to just under a boil. Add the coconut milk and warm through (but don't let boil, or it will curdle). Serve, garnished with fresh coriander.

Carrot Ginger Soup

I learned to love this soup when I lived in London. On those cold and rainy days it was a really great way to perk up. The ginger gives you a kick-start and the smoothness of the carrot warms your belly.

Ingredients

60 g (2 ¼ oz) unsalted butter
1 large white onion, chopped
2 tablespoons fresh ginger, peeled, and
finely chopped
2 garlic cloves, minced
600 g (1 lb 5 oz) carrots, peeled, chopped
750 ml (26 fl oz) water
1 vegetable stock cube
salt and black pepper
4 tablespoons sour cream
a few sprigs fresh coriander (cilantro)

Method

In a heavy saucepan, melt the butter over low heat. Add the onion and sauté 4 minutes, or until translucent. Add the ginger and garlic, and sauté for 3 minutes. Add the carrots, sauté 1 minute, and add the water and stock cube. Bring to a boil. Lower the heat, partially cover the pan, and simmer until the carrots are very tender, about 20 minutes. Remove from the heat and let cool slightly.

Purée the soup in batches, in a blender or with a handheld mixer. Return the soup to the pan, and season with some salt and black pepper. To serve, ladle the soup into bowls, and top each with a spoonful of sour cream and a sprinkling of fresh coriander.

This soup is great in summer and winter. Black beans are bursting in flavour on their own, but this combination adds even more zest to their smoky taste. Let this soup transport you to the beaches of Brazil.

Black Bean, Orange and Chilli Soup

Ingredients

300 g (10 ½ oz) dried black beans, soaked in cold water for at least 3 hours, or overnight

4 tablespoons olive oil

1 large white onion, chopped

2 garlic cloves, chopped

2 teaspoons chilli powder

3 teaspoons ground cumin

500 ml (17 fl oz) water

1 vegetable stock cube

2 tins tomatoes, with juices

2 oranges, juice and zest

2 Grilled Peppers (red ones; see recipe, page 26)

salt and black pepper

4 tablespoons Greek yoghurt

a few sprigs fresh coriander (cilantro) or parsley

Method

Drain the beans, transfer to a saucepan and add 1 litre (35 fl oz) cold water. Bring to a boil, then reduce the heat and simmer for 1 hour. Check for tenderness. Drain and set aside.

Place a heavy saucepan over low-medium heat. Add the olive oil, and sauté the onions, garlic, chilli powder and cumin until the onions are translucent; don't let them brown. Add the water, stock cube, tomatoes, beans and the orange juice and slowly bring to just below the boil. Lower the heat and simmer 10 minutes.

Meanwhile, chop the peppers into 2 cm (³/₄ inch) pieces. Add these, and half the orange zest, to the soup a few minutes before serving.

Serve in bowls, with a dollop of the yoghurt, and garnished with fresh coriander or parsley and the remaining orange zest.

The Big Guys

When I started Small World most take-away places only provided typical 'fast food' dishes. I wanted to provide restaurant-style food, but with a home-cooked twist. These mains all work well as simple family meals, but they will impress your guests, too!

Aussie Beef Pies

Meat pies are to Australians what hamburgers are to Americans and croquettes are to the Dutch. They are a national staple and come in many varieties, from cheap 'fast food' versions to those you buy at high-quality pastry shops. But one thing you can be sure of: Australians will always enjoy them with a healthy dousing of ketchup. So when I started my shop, meat pies were a must-have and this is the version we came up with. The beef and vegetable mix is best made the day before. This allows the flavours to blend and also makes it easier to put the filling into the pastries.

Ingredients

1.5 kg (3 lb 5 oz) minced beef, not too lean
2 tablespoons olive oil
200 g (7 oz) carrots, cut in 1 cm ($\frac{1}{2}$ inch) pieces
100 g (3 $\frac{1}{2}$ oz) celery, cut in 1 cm ($\frac{1}{2}$ inch) pieces
100 g (3 $\frac{1}{2}$ oz) onions, chopped
1 beef or chicken stock cube, crumbled
150 g (5 $\frac{1}{2}$ oz) frozen peas
100 g (3 $\frac{1}{2}$ oz) courgettes (zucchini), cut in 1 cm ($\frac{1}{2}$ inch) pieces
100 g (3 $\frac{1}{2}$ oz) green peppers (capsicums), cut in 1 cm ($\frac{1}{2}$ inch) pieces
600 g (1 lb 5 oz) chopped tomatoes (tins are fine)
300 g (10 $\frac{1}{2}$ oz) tomato sauce for pasta (tomato passata or *coulis*)
1 $\frac{1}{2}$ tablespoons ketchup (tomato sauce)
1 $\frac{1}{2}$ tablespoons Worcestershire Sauce
2 teaspoons paprika
2 teaspoons granulated onion
$\frac{3}{4}$ teaspoon salt
$\frac{3}{4}$ teaspoon freshly ground black pepper
720 g (1 lb 9 oz) good-quality puff pastry (you will need sixteen 13x13 cm (5 inch) squares of pastry)
2 eggs, beaten

Method

Place a large saucepan over medium heat. When hot, add the minced beef and brown well, about 10 minutes. Drain in a colander. Add the oil to the pan, then the carrot and celery. Cook until al dente, about 5 minutes. Add the onion and the stock cube and cook for 2 minutes. Add the peas, sauté a couple of minutes, then add the courgette and peppers. Cook for 5 minutes, then return the beef to the pan. Stir in the tomatoes and pasta sauce and simmer for 10 minutes. Add the ketchup and Worcestershire Sauce, stir to mix, then add the paprika, granulated onion, salt and pepper, and simmer for another 10 minutes. Remove from the heat, cool to room temperature, and refrigerate until cold.

Preheat the oven to 175°C (350°F). Roll out the puff pastry to about 5 mm ($\frac{1}{4}$ inch) thick. Use a bread and butter plate as a stencil to create two rounds for the pie tins, one for the bottom and sides and one for the top. Line eight round pie tins (3 cm/1 $\frac{1}{4}$ inches deep and 9 cm/3 $\frac{1}{2}$ inches diametre) with pastry. Divide the beef mixture amongst the pies. Brush the pastry edges with a little egg, lay the second pastry round on top, and gently press together. The egg will act as your glue. Brush the top of the pies with the remaining egg, to make a nice glaze, and pop into the oven for 25 minutes, or until golden brown. Serve with lashings of ketchup.

In general, I'm not really a fan of quiches, especially not of the flat flan-style ones. However, this quiche is the bomb. The combination of sweetly roasted squash with creamy goat's cheese and the earthiness of nutmeg make this an unforgettable taste and texture experience. What I always find absurd about this recipe is the small number of eggs, but they are just enough to hold together the copious amount of creamy goat's cheese. It's best to make this quiche a day in advance and cut it into slices when cold.

Makes 10 generous slices.

Roasted Pumpkin and French Goat's Cheese Quiche

Ingredients

For the dough
200 g (7 oz) cold butter, unsalted, cut into small cubes
400 g (14 oz) plain (all-purpose) flour, sifted
1 1/2 teaspoons salt
1 1/2 teaspoons sugar (optional)
1 small egg, beaten
60 g (2 1/4 oz) sour cream
water, as needed

For the filling
1 small pumpkin or butternut squash, peeled, and chopped into 3 cm (1 1/4 inch) cubes
2 tablespoons olive oil
1/2 teaspoon finely grated nutmeg
salt and black pepper
1 medium head broccoli, separated into florets
2 tablespoons unsalted butter

1 medium white onion, chopped
4 large eggs
250 g (9 oz) sour cream
250 ml (9 fl oz) double (thick) cream
1 tablespoon granulated onion
200 g (7 oz) Emmental or Swiss cheese, grated
350 g (12 oz) French goat's cheese, such as soft French chèvre

Method

To make the dough: using the pastry attachment, mix all the ingredients except the water together in a food processor. Or, mix with a fork in a large bowl, so as not to melt the butter. The less you work the dough, the better the result. If your pastry seems dry, just add a few teaspoons of water, little by little, until you have the desired consistency. Cover the dough in plastic wrap and refrigerate.

Preheat the oven to 175°C (350°F). To make the filling, arrange the pumpkin in a medium roasting tin. Add the olive oil, sprinkle with half the nutmeg, pepper and salt, and toss together to coat. Pop this into the oven for 20 minutes. Don't worry about it being completely cooked because it will cook again inside the quiche and you want it to have some bite. Lightly steam the broccoli until al dente. In a saucepan, melt the butter over a low heat and sauté the onions until translucent, about 6 minutes.

In a large bowl that can be used with a hand-held blender, add the eggs, sour cream, double cream, granulated onion, the remaining nutmeg, and salt and pepper. Blend this all together.

Now you're ready to assemble the quiche. Line a 26 cm (10 ½ inch) spring-form tin with baking paper. On a lightly floured surface, roll out the dough to the proportions of the tin and place it into the tin. Use your fingers to push the dough up the tin sides, as needed, with an overlap of 5 cm (2 inches). Don't be too fussy, as a rustic crust on top will look nice.

Preheat the oven to 175°C (350°F). Sprinkle the dough-base with half the Emmental cheese.

Arrange half the roasted squash and half the broccoli over the cheese. Roughly crumble the goat's cheese over the vegetables, making sure to leave large pieces of cheese. Add the rest of the roasted squash and broccoli, and top with the sautéed onions. Pour the egg and cream mix over the layers. Sprinkle the remaining Emmental over the top, and fold over the sides of the dough toward the centre. Dip a pastry brush into the filling, and glaze the top of the quiche. Place on an oven rack in the middle of the oven, and bake for 1 ½ hours. Be not afraid, the quiche is done, and once the cheese has cooled, it will firm up. Let the quiche cool to room temperature (this will take several hours), then refrigerate until cold. Only then can it easily be cut into slices.

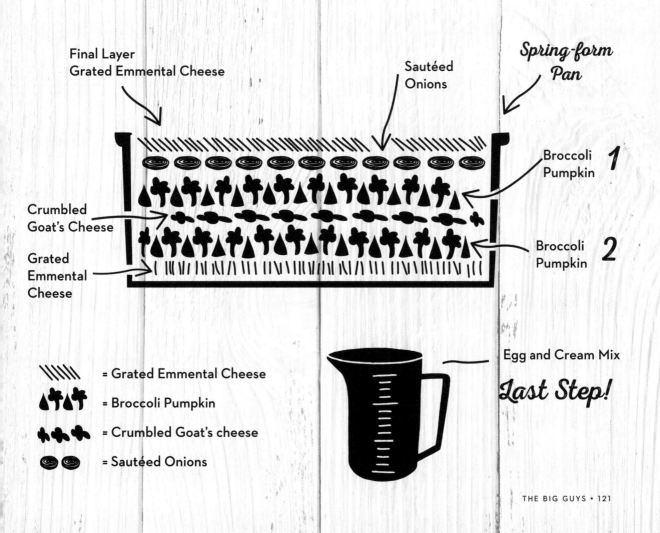

Final Layer Grated Emmental Cheese

Sautéed Onions

Spring-form Pan

Broccoli Pumpkin 1

Crumbled Goat's Cheese

Grated Emmental Cheese

Broccoli Pumpkin 2

\\\\\ = Grated Emmental Cheese

♦♠♣ = Broccoli Pumpkin

♣♣♣ = Crumbled Goat's cheese

◉◉ = Sautéed Onions

Egg and Cream Mix

Last Step!

THAI-STYLE Fish Cakes

WITH SALMON AND COD

Thai food hasn't become one of the world's 'number one' cuisines without reason. Its sublime tropical flavours rule. Thai fish cake recipes have delicious flavours, but can often be on the rubbery side and rather flimsy and small. So we took their spices and herbs and added them instead to fresh salmon and cod fillets, to create a more robust and juicy cake. *Thai-Style Fish Cakes* have become a huge favourite in our shop, served as a main with the Haricots Verts Salad with Roasted Walnuts and Parmesan Shavings (see recipe, page 97) and in the *Thai-Style Fish Cakes with Avocado and Wasabi Mayo* sandwich (see recipe, page 91). Makes approximately 12 fish cakes.

Ingredients

40 g (1 1/2 oz) ginger, finely chopped
2 garlic cloves, finely chopped
1 medium red chilli pepper, trimmed, leaving seeds intact, and chopped
2 lime leaves, stalk and midrib removed, very finely chopped,
1 large stalk celery, finely chopped
1 green pepper (capsicum), cut into small cubes
2 French shallots, chopped
40 g (1 1/2 oz) lemon grass (*sereh*), end removed, and super-finely chopped
1/4 bunch fresh coriander (cilantro), stalks and leaves, super-finely chopped
300 g (10 1/2 oz) fresh salmon, skinned and boned, half lightly mashed, half in small pieces
300 g (10 1/2 oz) fresh cod, lightly mashed
30 g (1 oz) green beans (haricots verts), chopped into very small rounds
1 tablespoon Thai fish sauce
a pinch coarsely ground black pepper
as needed vegetable oil

Method

Place the ginger, garlic, chilli pepper, lime leaves, celery, green pepper, shallots and lemon grass in a food processor bowl. Blitz together until well mixed but not a paste. Transfer to a large bowl and add the fresh coriander, salmon, cod, green beans, fish sauce and pepper. Mix together, taking care to keep some of the fish chunky.

Preheat the oven to 175°C (350°F). Place a large pan over medium heat, and add enough oil to cover the bottom by 2 cm (3/4 inch). Using an ice cream scoop or similar, drop each cake carefully in the hot oil and brown on both sides until golden, about 2 minutes each side. Transfer the fish cakes to a wire rack set on top of an oven dish, and bake 10 minutes. Sweet chilli sauce goes perfectly with these little morsels. Do you have any extra fish cakes? See our *Thai-Style Fish Cakes with Avocado and Wasabi Mayo* sandwich recipe.

This Tex Mex-style burrito arrived on our menu over a decade ago. It's one of the most popular dishes we have and we can't make them fast enough. Hearty and spicy, they really satisfy every craving. We serve them with a side of sour cream, for extra decadence. It's best to prepare the mix a few hours ahead, or even the day before, because a cold mix is much easier to work with.
Makes 4 large burritos.

Hearty Lamb Burrito

Ingredients

500 g (1 lb 2 oz) minced lamb
4 tablespoons olive oil
2 peppers (capsicums), different colours
2 medium onions, chopped
2 garlic cloves, peeled and chopped
1 large stalk celery, chopped
1 medium courgette (zucchini), chopped
40 g (1 ½ oz) frozen corn
50 g (1 ¾ oz) black olives, pitted and crushed
4 tablespoons sliced jalapeños, drained
400 g (14 oz) tinned kidney beans, drained
200 g (7 oz) tinned chopped tomatoes
200 g (7 oz) tomato sauce for pasta (tomato passata or coulis)
½ teaspoon ground coriander
¾ teaspoon ground cumin
¾ teaspoon paprika
¾ teaspoon granulated onion
¼ teaspoon ground cinnamon
½ teaspoon coarsely ground black pepper
⅓ teaspoon sea salt
½ tablespoon cocoa powder
¼ bunch fresh coriander (cilantro), chopped
4 large (30 cm/12 inch) flour tortillas
250 g (9 oz) Cheddar cheese, grated
sour cream (optional)

Method

Place a large saucepan over medium heat. When hot, add the minced lamb and brown well, about 10 minutes. Drain in a colander and set aside. Add 3 tablespoons of the olive oil to the pan, then the peppers, onions, garlic, celery and courgette and cook until the onions are translucent. Add the corn, olives, jalapeños and kidney beans, stir to mix, and simmer for 5 minutes. Add the tomatoes and pasta sauce, but keep a little sauce for later, and simmer another 15 minutes. Transfer the mixture to a bowl and set aside. Add the remaining olive oil to the pan, then the ground coriander, cumin, paprika, granulated onion, cinnamon, pepper and salt, and sauté for a few minutes. Add the lamb mixture to the pan, let everything simmer together over low heat for another 10 minutes, then mix in the vegetables. Add the cocoa and the fresh coriander. Set aside to completely cool.

Preheat the oven to 175°C (350°F). It can be quite tricky to wrap up a burrito but, with practice, you can learn how to do it. Just do your best, and remember–you can always hide any mistakes by turning it upside down!

To begin, sprinkle about 20 g (¾ oz) of the Cheddar cheese across the middle of each tortilla. Ladle on some of the filling, just below the centre of the tortilla. Fold in two sides by about 5 cm (2 inches). With your thumbs, bring up the bottom of the tortilla to cover the centre, and tuck in the ends. Repeat with the remaining tortillas. Spread pasta sauce on top. Sprinkle the burritos with the remaining cheese, and bake 15 minutes. Serve warm, with sour cream if liked.

Spicy Veggie Burrito

Make as the *Lamb Burrito*, but omit the lamb. This burrito will be a lot spicier as it doesn't have the same volume as the lamb burrito. If you'd like it to be less spicy, adjust the quantities to your taste. We also like to add black beans to this mix. Serve with a side of chopped avocado and, of course, some sour cream.

1

2

3

4

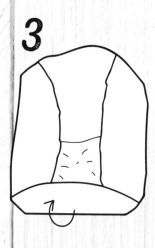
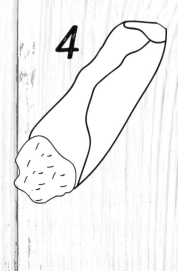

Spanish Tortilla with Sweet Potato

The Spanish might find calling this a tortilla outrageous, because they are very proud of this national dish. We spice it up and add all kinds of ingredients, from sun-dried tomatoes and olives to grilled courgettes and capers. We find that baking the potatoes gives a less oily result than pan-frying, and we also like to finish the tortilla in the oven, unlike the traditional method where it's made only on top of the stove. The following recipe is the most popular, but feel free to play around with it.
Serves 10.

Ingredients

500 g (1 lb 2 oz) potatoes, cut into 5 mm (¹/₄ inch) slices
500 g (1 lb 2 oz) sweet potatoes, cut into 5 mm (¹/₄ inch) slices
1 small white onion, cut into 5 mm (¹/₄ inch) slices
8 tablespoons olive oil
sea salt and freshly ground black pepper
15 large eggs, beaten
1 tablespoon granulated onion
150 g (5 ¹/₂ oz) chopped veggies, such as sautéed peppers (capsicums), peas and mushrooms

Method

Preheat the oven to 175°C (350°F). In a large roasting tin, toss the potatoes, sweet potatoes and onion in the olive oil, and sprinkle with salt. Cover the tin with baking paper, seal with kitchen foil, and bake 50 minutes. Remove from the oven and set aside, still covered, for 15 minutes.

Remove the potatoes from the tin with a slotted spoon, and reserve the oil to use later. Let the potatoes cool. Lightly beat the eggs together with some salt, black pepper and the onion powder. Add the potatoes and the chopped veggies. Heat a large pan (28 or 30 cm/11 ¹/₄ or 12 inches) and add some of the reserved oil. When almost smoking, add the egg mixture To avoid any sticking, shake loose from the edge of the pan. Lower the heat, cover with a lid, and cook for 10 minutes. Carefully flip the eggs over onto a large, flat plate. Return the pan to the heat, add more of the reserved oil, and carefully slide the tortilla back into the pan. Cook on high for a couple of minutes to seal the outside. Reduce the heat to low and cook for another 10 minutes. Transfer the tortilla to a flat ovenproof plate and bake 8 minutes. Let cool for at least 30 minutes before cutting.

My hometown of Melbourne boasts the largest population of Greeks outside of Athens in the whole world, so I was fortunate to grow up surrounded by Greek culture and of course, the country's amazing cuisine. There are so many variations on this dish but, as a Greek friend of mine once told me, spanakopita just means spinach pie, so add to it what you will. Spanakopita is often made with phyllo, which is delicious, but we chose to use a more hearty, rustic pastry. If you want, you can sprinkle sesame seeds on top before baking, for a little extra crunch.
Makes 6 pies.

Spanakopita

Ingredients

For the filling
2 tablespoons olive oil
1/2 bunch fresh dill, chopped
1 1/2 large leeks, white and tender green
parts only, chopped
3 spring onions (scallions), chopped
500 g (1 lb 2 oz) spinach, frozen
salt and black pepper
375 g (13 oz) feta cheese
2 medium eggs, beaten

For the pastry
500 g (1 lb 2 oz) plain (all-purpose) flour, sifted
1/2 teaspoon salt
4 tablespoons olive oil
250 ml (8 fl oz) water
1 tablespoon white wine vinegar
2 large eggs, beaten
sesame seeds (optional)

Method

Preheat the oven to 175°C (350°F).

Heat the 2 tablespoons olive oil in a pan and sauté the dill, leeks and spring onions over medium heat. Add the spinach and cover, leaving over low heat to defrost the spinach, about 10 minutes, then stir together. Season to taste. Once the filling has cooled, crumble the feta into the mixture and fold in the eggs.

For the pastry, pile the flour on the work surface and make a hole in the middle: you want it to look like a little volcano. Put the salt, olive oil, water and white wine vinegar in the crater and knead it all together until you have a good texture to roll out. Roll the dough out to 2.5 mm (1/8 inch).

Using a plate of about 22 cm (8 1/2 inches), cut out 6 circles of dough. Brush the edge of the circle with half of the egg. Separate your spinach mixture into 6 portions. Lay the mixture on the lower half of each circle, leaving the edges clear, and fold the upper half of the pastry on top. Press the sides together using a fork. Brush the tops with the remaining egg.

Place the spanakopitas on a baking tray lined with baking paper, and bake in the oven for 25 minutes, or until golden brown.

Pastry

Spinach
Filling

Sesame

Portobello Mushrooms
WITH SWEET POTATO AND TALEGGIO

I completely love these. They are a good meat replacement, so make a great choice for the vegetarian clients. They also make an excellent side dish. I make a more standard version with goat's cheese and roasted peppers, but our Icelandic chef, Salka, came up with this really original and truly delicious recipe. They have quickly become one of the favourites in the shop. Makes 8.

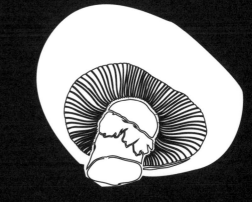

Ingredients

1.5 kg (3 lb 5 oz) sweet potatoes, peeled and cut into 4×4 cm (1 ½ inch) cubes
4 tablespoons olive oil
4 tablespoons granulated onion
salt and black pepper
4 garlic cloves, peeled
4 tomatoes, cored, and sliced in half
½ teaspoon dried thyme
40 g (1 ½ oz) butter
8 portobello mushrooms, cleaned, with stalks removed
4 sprigs parsley, leaves only, chopped
160 g (5 ½ oz) Taleggio cheese, cut into 8 strips

Method

Preheat the oven to 180°C (350°F). In a large bowl, toss together the sweet potatoes, 3 tablespoons of the olive oil, the granulated onion, salt and pepper, and add one of the garlic cloves. Transfer to a baking tray, and spread evenly. Bake 25 minutes, or until nicely browned. Set aside.

Place the 8 tomato halves, face-up, on a baking tray, and drizzle with the remaining olive oil. Sprinkle with the thyme, salt and pepper, and pop into the oven for 30 minutes.

Mash the sweet potatoes with the butter and a few pinches of parsley. Season to taste. Separate the mash into 8 portions, and divide it over the 8 mushrooms. Top each with a roasted half-tomato, face up, then a slice of Taleggio cheese. Chop the remaining garlic clove with the rest of the parsley, and sauté in the remaining olive oil until the garlic is soft. Spoon this mixture over the cheese, and season with salt and pepper. Bake 15 minutes, or until the cheese has melted and is a nice golden brown.

Lentils taste just great on their own: they have their own satisfying, delicious flavour from mother nature. However, when you spice them up with this lasagne filling and top it off with a creamy béchamel, you're in for a treat.
Serves 6.

Spicy Lentil Lasagne
WITH CREAMY BÉCHAMEL

Ingredients

300 g (10 ½ oz) green lentils, soaked for
at least 3 hours
2 tablespoons olive oil
1 small white onion, peeled, and diced
3 garlic cloves, finely chopped
1 stalk celery, finely chopped
1 medium carrot, finely chopped
1 red pepper (capsicum), finely chopped
1 tomato, chopped
12 sun-dried tomatoes, packed in olive oil,
finely chopped
4 chilli peppers, deseeded, and finely chopped
1 tin tomatoes, with juices, chopped
8 basil leaves, roughly chopped
125 ml (4 fl oz) water
salt and black pepper

Béchamel sauce
3 tablespoons butter
40 g (1 ½ oz) plain (all-purpose) flour
550 ml (19 fl oz) milk
¼ teaspoon nutmeg, freshly ground
a handful grated gruyère, Swiss
cheese or Emmental

12 lasagne sheets
a handful finely grated Parmesan cheese

Method

Place the lentils in a pan with 750 ml (26 fl oz) water, and bring to a boil. Reduce the heat, and simmer 25 minutes. Drain, and set aside.

Set a large saucepan over medium heat, add the olive oil, then the onion, garlic, celery, carrot, pepper, tomato, sun-dried tomatoes and chilli pepper. Fry until soft, but don't let the vegetables brown. This should take about 15 minutes. Add the lentils and tinned tomatoes, basil and the 125 ml (4 fl oz) of water, and continue cooking for 15 minutes. Add salt and pepper to taste.

In a smaller, heavy saucepan, melt the butter over medium heat. Slowly add the flour, until you have a mixture like wet sand. Cook for a couple of minutes, lower the heat, and slowly add a little of the milk, stirring constantly, to make a roux (butter-flour mix). Add the rest of the milk, little by little, continuing to stir until the sauce thickens. Add salt, pepper and the nutmeg, and whisk in the cheese.

Preheat the oven to 175°C (350°F). Have your béchamel sauce, tomato-lentil filling and the lasagne sheets ready.

In a lasagne dish (or similar), spread a few big dollops of the lentil mix over the bottom, and lightly cover with lasagne sheets. Cover with a third of the béchamel sauce and half of the remaining lentil mix. Repeat again, layering lasagne sheets, béchamel and lentil mix, and then add the final layer of lasagne sheets. Pour over the remaining third of béchamel, and sprinkle with the Parmesan cheese. Tightly cover the dish with kitchen foil, and bake 35 minutes. Remove the foil, and return the lasagne to the oven for 10 minutes, to brown.

Serve with a fresh green salad.

The Lasagne

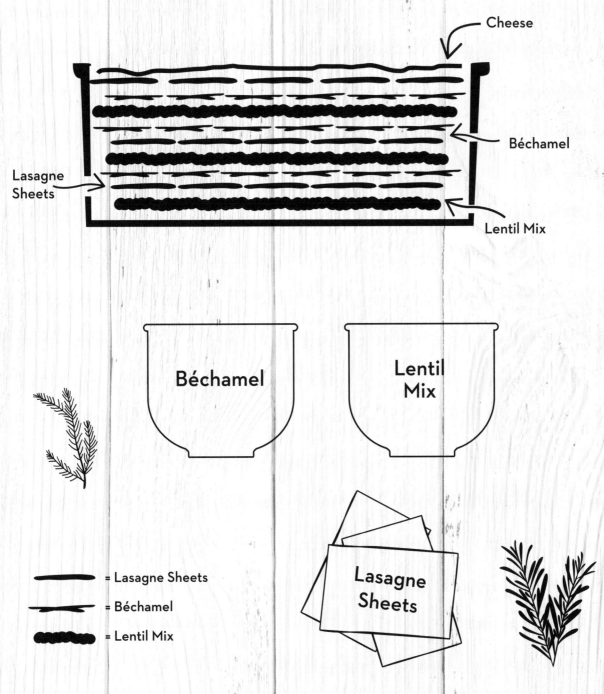

Cheese

Béchamel

Lasagne
Sheets

Lentil Mix

Béchamel

Lentil
Mix

Lasagne
Sheets

⎯⎯⎯ = Lasagne Sheets

⎯⎯ = Béchamel

●●●● = Lentil Mix

Chicken Fillet in a Mustard Cream Sauce

The staff have contributed to this book with a number of recipes. This is another one of Salka's. At Small World we make many chicken dishes, but this one is continually voted one of the best in the shop. On a dark and cold Amsterdam evening, this creamy Parmesan sauce with just a bite of mustard and pesto will certainly warm you up.
Serves 4.

Ingredients

2 medium leeks, tough dark-green parts discarded
6 tablespoons olive oil
2 garlic cloves, chopped
1 tablespoon wholegrain mustard
1 tablespoon Pesto (see recipe, page 18)
1 teaspoon mustard powder
500 ml (17 fl oz) double (thick) cream
2 tablespoons parsley, chopped
1 teaspoon salt
1 tablespoon coarsely ground black pepper
4 chicken fillets, each about 125 g (4 ½ oz)
100 g (3 ½ oz) Parmesan cheese, grated
50 g (1 ¾ oz) Parmesan cheese, shaved

Method

Preheat the oven to 175°C (350°F). Slice the leeks in 1.5 cm ($^5/_8$ inch) rounds. Wash well in a colander, and shake dry. Warm 2 tablespoons of the olive oil in a saucepan set over low heat, add the leeks, and cook 5 minutes. Add the garlic, and cook another 4 minutes; don't let brown. Add the wholegrain mustard, pesto and mustard powder, stir together, and simmer 3 minutes. Add the cream, half the parsley, and salt and pepper to taste. Continue simmering for 10 to 15 minutes, or until it starts to thicken up nicely.

While the sauce is simmering away, heat a large pan or a chargrill pan or plate. Sear each chicken fillet individually in 1 tablespoon of olive oil. You only need to brown them, the cooking will take place in the oven.

Arrange the fillets in a deep oven dish, cover with the sauce, and sprinkle over the grated Parmesan. Bake 15 to 20 minutes, or until the fillets are cooked through. To serve, garnish with the Parmesan shavings and remaining parsley.

Nothing beats the lovely smell of baking. The recipes in this chapter are all finger-licking good and with a bonus: all freeze really well. So there is no excuse to not start baking immediately and generously.

Small World's legendary Carrot Cake has made it into guidebooks around the world. This is the most popular (and secret!) recipe in the shop. So it was hard to share. The moist cake, made luscious with a generous amount of coconut and pineapple, topped with a cream-cheese frosting and doused with roasted almonds, make it deliciously addictive. Serves 12.

Our Legendary
Carrot Cake

Ingredients

For the cake
550 g (1 lb 4 oz) caster (superfine) sugar
360 ml (12 fl oz) vegetable oil
3 large eggs
1 tablespoon vanilla extract
360 g (12 ³/₄ oz) plain (all-purpose) flour
3 ¹/₂ teaspoons bicarbonate of soda (baking soda)
1 ¹/₄ teaspoons fine salt
1 teaspoon ground cinnamon
¹/₃ teaspoon nutmeg
¹/₄ teaspoon ground allspice
300 g (10 ¹/₂ oz) carrots, finely grated
200 g (7 oz) flaked coconut
240 g (8 ¹/₂ oz) pineapple pieces (fresh is best, but tinned is fine, too)

For the frosting
400 g (14 oz) cream cheese
60 ml (2 fl oz) single (thin/pouring) cream
1 teaspoon vanilla extract
75 g (2 ¹/₂ oz) icing (confectioners') sugar
6 tablespoons toasted flaked almonds

Method

Preheat the oven to 175°C (350°F). Beat together the sugar and vegetable oil until light and fluffy. Add the eggs and vanilla extract, and beat well. Sift together the flour, bicarbonate of soda, salt, cinnamon, nutmeg and allspice, and fold into the wet mixture. Then fold in the grated carrot, flaked coconut and crushed pineapple. Folding is important here, to keep the cake light and fluffy. Over-mixing will make it rubbery.

Grease a 28 cm (11 ¹/₄ inch) round spring-form tin. Cut baking paper to fit on to the bottom and up the sides of the tin, and place it in. Pour the batter into the tin and bake for 1 hour. Remove the cake from the oven, and insert a toothpick into the centre to check if done. If the toothpick comes out clean, the cake is ready. Let the cake cool for at least 2 hours before removing from the tin.

Cut the cake horizontally in half with a thin, serrated knife. Open the cake so the cut sides are face-up.

Meanwhile, prepare the frosting. In a mixing bowl, blend the cream cheese, cream, vanilla and icing sugar. Place a generous dollop in the centre of one side of the cake and, with a spatula, spread it in a 1 cm (¹/₂ inch) thick layer outwards, to the sides. Stop 1 cm (¹/₂ inch) from the edges. Place the second side of the cake, cut side down, on top, and press down until the frosting appears at the edges. Cover the top and sides of the cake with the remaining frosting. Sprinkle the sides and some of the top of the cake with the almonds, leaving a nice white centre.

Note: Make the cake the day before. It's easier to spread the frosting when it's completely cold.

CLASSIC
New York Cheesecake

Cheesecakes come in so many varieties and forms, from caramel to cherry. However, the 'New York classic cheesecake' is my favourite. The spiced and crumbly base, topped with a luscious creamy filling that has just a touch of lemon, makes it subtly divine. Serves 12.

Ingredients

For the base

185 g (6 ¹/₂ oz) graham crackers or similar cookies

60 g (2 ¹/₄ oz) butter, cut into cubes

³/₄ teaspoon ground cinnamon

¹/₄ teaspoon ground allspice

¹/₄ teaspoon nutmeg

50 g (1 ³/₄ oz) dark brown sugar

For the filling

Everything should be at room temperature, even the lemons

750 g (1 lb 10oz) cream cheese

250 g (9 oz) caster (superfine) sugar

¹/₂ teaspoon lemon zest

2 teaspoons lemon juice

3 large eggs

³/₄ teaspoon vanilla extract

100 g (3 ¹/₂ oz) plain (all-purpose) flour, sifted

¹/₄ teaspoon bicarbonate of soda (baking soda)

375 g (13 oz) sour cream

Method

Preheat the oven to 200°C (400°F). In a food processor, mix together all of the ingredients for the base until well-combined, but don't turn it into a paste. Transfer the mixture to a 26 cm (10 ¹/₂ inch) spring-form tin and gently press into the bottom and sides. Bake for 12 minutes. Remove from the oven. Turn the oven down to 150°C (300°F).

Make the filling. With an electric mixer, beat the cream cheese until smooth. Beat in the sugar and, with a spatula, wipe down the sides of the bowl several times, to mix everything together. Add the lemon zest and lemon juice, eggs and vanilla extract, and cream together. Add the flour and bicarbonate of soda and mix until smooth. Make sure there are no lumps. Then add the sour cream. Mix this all together until well combined.

Ladle spoonfuls of the mixture onto the middle of the tin base. Sprinkle some of the crumbs from the base to the sides of the tin to create the cake's edge, then spread the mixture over the base. Place a tin filled with water in the oven, to keep the air moist. Put the cake on the middle shelf of the oven and bake 30 minutes. Turn off the oven, open the door, and leave the cake to cool slowly in the oven. When cold, refrigerate.

To serve, bring the cake to room temperature. For easy slicing, first dip your knife into boiling water.

A lemon tart is up there among my favourite desserts, so I always order it wherever I go. In Italy, it's called *torta al limone*. Here, it's more commonly known by its French name, *tarte au citron*. A good lemon tart should have a crumbly base and a sharp 'lemon attack' with a hint of creamy sweetness. The secret to the crumbly base is the hard-boiled egg yolk trick. I think of it as a summer dessert, but it's the perfect finale to any meal thanks to its tanginess.

Serves 12.

FRENCH Lemon Tart

Ingredients

For the pastry
280 g (10 oz) plain (all-purpose) flour, sifted
50 g (1 ³/₄ oz) caster (superfine) sugar
¹/₄ teaspoon fine salt
170 g (6 oz) unsalted butter
2 eggs, hard-boiled
1 egg

For the filling
2 lemons, strained juice and grated zest
3 eggs
150 g (5 ¹/₂ oz) caster (superfine) sugar
60 g (2 ¹/₄ oz) unsalted butter, softened

Method

For the pastry, sift the dry ingredients together in a large bowl. Remove the yolks from the hard-boiled eggs and discard the whites. Push the yolks through a fine sieve with a spoon to create a sandy-coloured powder. Add to the dry ingredients, then add the egg and whisk everything together. Don't over-mix. If you use a kitchen mixer, the hook attachment works best for this. Refrigerate for a few hours, or overnight.

Preheat the oven to 175°C (350°F). On a lightly floured surface, roll out the pastry to fit a fluted, 26 cm (10 ¹/₂ inch) round tart tin, preferably with a removable bottom. Press the pastry into the pan to about 1 cm (¹/₂ inch) thick, then press it up the sides of the tin with your fingers. Cut out a piece of baking paper larger than the bottom of the tart tin, and place it over the pastry. Weight it down by spreading a generous quantity of pebbles, beans or coins on top - whatever you have available. Bake for 20 minutes and remove from the oven. Remove the baking paper by folding up the sides all at one time, so the weights don't drop into the pastry.

To make the lemon filling, place all the filling ingredients in the bowl of a double boiler (bain-marie). Whisk constantly to ensure the egg whites don't separate before being incorporated into the mixture. When nicely thickened, remove from the heat and pour into the pie pastry. If you have any left over, store in a glass jar in the fridge. It's great on pancakes. Bake until golden, about 30 minutes. Cool to room temperature, then transfer to the refrigerator, to chill.

Note: It's best to make the lemon tart the day before, as it needs time to cool down properly.

Rich Fudge Brownies

As Small World is directly across the street from one of Amsterdam's renowned coffee shops, brownies come to mind as an obvious offering. There are so many kinds of brownies out there. But we make a rich fudge brownie that has actually become famous in town and has even been sent all over the world. The high sugar content makes sure that the brownies keep well. They freeze perfectly and they are dynamite served slightly warmed with a scoop of vanilla ice cream.
Makes 20.

Ingredients

270 g (9 ½ oz) plain (all-purpose) flour, sifted
2 teaspoons fine salt
450 g (1 lb) unsalted butter
260 g (9 ¼ oz) dark chocolate (70%-85%)
800 g (1 lb 12 oz) caster (superfine) sugar
2 teaspoons vanilla extract
8 eggs

For the glaze
400 g (14 oz) dark chocolate (70%-85%)
125 ml (4 fl oz) double (thick) cream

Method

Preheat the oven to 175°C (350°F). Sift flour and salt together into a medium-size bowl and set aside. In a double boiler (bain-marie), melt the butter and 260 g (9 ¼ oz) chocolate. Chocolate is very sensitive, so make sure not to over-heat it. Add half the sugar and the vanilla extract, and mix together. In a kitchen mixer, beat the eggs and remaining sugar for 1 minute on high, then add to the chocolate mixture. Mix together until you have a thick, glossy, chocolatey batter.

Grease the sides and bottom of a 23x33 cm (9x13 inch) brownie tin and line with baking paper. Pour the batter into the tin, then bang the tin a few times on the counter to release any air bubbles. Place the tin in the middle of the oven, and bake for 35 minutes. It's difficult to gauge the doneness of these brownies since they should be gooey in the centre. So have faith, and leave them to cool and set. When completely cooled, flip the tin over so that the flat bottom is now the top. Gently peel away the baking paper. This is easier to do if you've refrigerated the brownies for a few hours.

To make the glaze, melt the chocolate in a double boiler until just melted, and remove from heat. Gently and slowly fold in the cream without over mixing. Now you need to work more quickly, to make sure the glazing doesn't harden too soon. Pour the glaze into the centre of the top of the brownies, and work it out to the edges with a spatula. With any residual drips, seal the sides. Allow to cool, and slice into pieces.

This dessert is definitely the 'Southern Belle' of our repertoire. The chewy, sweet caramel with the crunchy, roasted pecans will make you say 'frankly my dear, I don't give a damn about the calories!' Serve it warm from the oven in the winter, with a scoop of vanilla ice cream.
Serves 8.

Pecan Pie

Ingredients

For the pastry
280 g (10 oz) plain (all-purpose) flour, sifted
50 g (1 ³/₄ oz) caster (superfine) sugar
¹/₄ teaspoon fine salt
170 g (6 oz) unsalted butter
2 eggs, hard-boiled
1 egg

For the filling
65 g (2 ¹/₄ oz) unsalted butter, softened
100 g (3 ¹/₂ oz) caster (superfine) sugar
100 g (3 ¹/₂ oz) golden caster or white caster (superfine) sugar
4 eggs
1 ¹/₂ tablespoons rum
1 ¹/₂ tablespoons vanilla extract
120 ml (4 fl oz) maple syrup
5 heaped handfuls pecans, unsalted

Method

Preheat the oven to 175°C (350°F). For the pastry, sift the dry ingredients together into a large bowl. Remove the yolks from the hard-boiled eggs and discard the whites. Push the yolks through a fine sieve with a spoon to create a sandy-coloured powder. Add to the dry ingredients, then add the egg and whisk everything together. Don't over-mix. If you use a kitchen mixer, the hook attachment works the best for this.

On a lightly floured surface, roll out the pastry to fit a fluted, 23 cm (9 inch) round tart tin, preferably with a removable bottom. Press the pastry into the tin to about 1 cm (¹/₂ inch) thick, then press it up into the sides of the tin with your fingers. Refrigerate for a few hours, or overnight.

For the filling, place the butter in a metal mixing bowl, let it soften, then whip by hand until smooth. Add both the sugars, whip again by hand, then add the eggs, rum, vanilla extract and maple syrup. Mix well, but not so that it gets foamy. Then add the pecans and mix well. Take the pastry out of the refrigerator, pour in the filling, and bake for 45 minutes.

Oatmeal Raisin Cookies

These Oatmeal Raisin Cookies remind me of the great cookies that we have in Australia to commemorate our memorial Anzac Day. Delicious and sweet, the oats give a bite to grind your teeth into. But the texture is still chewy and melts in your mouth. These are a daily hit in the café.
Makes 12.

Ingredients

170 g (6 oz) butter, softened
140 g (5 oz) caster (superfine) sugar
140 g (5 oz) golden caster or white caster (superfine) sugar
2 small eggs, beaten
1 teaspoon vanilla extract
160 g (5 ½ oz) plain (all-purpose) flour
1 teaspoon bicarbonate of soda (baking soda)
½ teaspoon ground cinnamon
¼ teaspoon fine salt
240 g (8 ½ oz) rolled (porridge) oats
70 g (2 ½ oz) large dark raisins

Method

Preheat the oven to 175°C (350°F). In a large bowl, whisk together the butter, caster sugar and golden caster sugar until smooth. Beat in the eggs and vanilla extract to make a smooth and fluffy mixture. Sift in the flour, bicarbonate of soda, cinnamon and salt, and gently mix together. Use a spoon, or a slower speed on the mixer. Fold in the oats and raisins.

We like to make large cookies, about 75 g (2 ½ oz) each. Scoop up some of the mixture with a spoon and, with your hand, form into a chunky, home-style cookie. Don't make them look too perfect, and be careful not to over-roll them. Line a baking tray with baking paper, arrange the cookies on it, and bake 13 minutes for a gooey cookie (which we like). If you prefer a more crunchy cookie, bake another 3 minutes. Let cool a little, and transfer to a wire rack. Let cool completely.

You can freeze this mixture: roll the dough into cookie balls, and freeze. Then you can raid the freezer when you want to, and have cookies ready-to-go in no time. Baking time for frozen dough is 17 minutes.

Years ago, on a busy Saturday morning in Small World, an American guy grabbed one of these and bit into it. He immediately started screaming 'OMG these cookies are the best, they're killer man! Killer, you hear!' Everyone cracked up laughing at his enthusiasm and, for many years, they were known as the 'killer cookies'. Bake a few, and find out why....
Makes 12.

Chocolate Chip Cookies

Ingredients

125 g (4 ¹/₂ oz) butter, softened
100 g (3 ¹/₂ oz) golden caster or white caster (superfine) sugar
100 g (3 ¹/₂ oz) caster (superfine) sugar
2 small eggs, lightly beaten
1 teaspoon vanilla extract
1 ¹/₂ teaspoons rum
225 g (8 oz) plain (all-purpose) flour
¹/₄ teaspoon fine salt
²/₃ teaspoon bicarbonate of soda (baking soda)
75 g (2 ¹/₂ oz) dried coconut, shredded
120 g (4 ¹/₄ oz) chocolate chips (we use a mix of milk, white and dark)

Method

Preheat the oven to 175°C (350°F). With a hand-held mixer, beat the butter, golden caster sugar and white caster sugar until light and fluffy. Add the eggs, vanilla extract and rum, and beat well. Sift in the flour, salt and bicarbonate of soda, and gently mix together. Fold in the grated coconut and chocolate chips.

Scoop up some of the mixture with a spoon and, with your hand, form into a chunky, home-style cookie (not 'perfect', like a shop-bought cookie). Line a baking tray with baking paper, arrange the cookies on it, and bake 13 minutes for a nice gooey texture. Cool slightly, until you can easily handle the cookies without them falling apart, and place on a wire rack to cool completely.

You can freeze this mixture: roll the dough into cookie balls, and freeze. Then you can raid the freezer when you want to, and have cookies ready-to-go in no time. Baking time for frozen dough is 17 minutes.

Muffins

In Small World, we use XL-size muffin tins, but you can use whatever size tins you have available. Be aware that, if you use smaller tins, you need to adjust the baking time accordingly. These muffin batters freeze well so, if you'd like to, you can double the mix, and freeze half for future use. Pull the mix out of the freezer the night before you want to bake.

These mixes can also be made with gluten-free flour. Don't over-mix the last stage, when you fold in the dry ingredients, as this will make the muffins rubbery. If you fold in gently, the wet ingredients will absorb nicely into the flour, so it's not necessary to beat the mix. Use a rubber spatula, and make sure to get well under the mix, to the bottom and the sides of the bowl, so there are no clumps. We use fluted muffin papers, but if you are in a pinch, baking paper cut in squares and folded into the muffin moulds work well, and actually look really cool and rustic. All recipes make 12 XL muffins.

Banana bread rocks, and I turned this into a muffin! When Small World first opened, I made these muffins with roasted walnuts. They always sold out. Then Francis arrived. A spicy, colourful character from Chicago, she frequented the café in her lust for good food. Francis loved everything, but she insisted I made this muffin with chocolate instead of walnuts. I argued the case for walnuts but, after a couple of days of her pleading, I finally gave in. She was thrilled with the result (her creation), the customers loved her enthusiasm and, by popular demand, the banana chocolate muffin was born. It's stayed with us for the last 15 years.

Play around with the recipe: try walnuts, chocolate, cinnamon, cardamom or combos. Use the very ripest bananas you can find–those that are well-yellowed or, better still, starting to blacken–as these have the best flavour.

Banana Chocolate Muffins

Ingredients

400 g (14 oz) plain (all-purpose) flour
1 ¹/₂ teaspoons baking powder
¹/₂ teaspoon bicarbonate of soda
(baking soda)
125 g (4 ¹/₂ oz) caster (superfine) sugar
¹/₂ teaspoon fine salt
4 large ripe bananas, mashed
2 eggs, lightly beaten
200 g (7 oz) butter, melted
150 g (5 ¹/₂ oz) chocolate
chips

Optional
75 g (2 ¹/₂ oz) walnuts, in pieces (and reduce
chocolate chips to 75 g/2 ¹/₂ oz)
1 ¹/₂ teaspoons ground cardamom or
ground cinnamon

Method

Preheat the oven to 175°C (350°F). In a large bowl, sift together the flour, baking powder, bicarbonate of soda, sugar and salt. In another large bowl, whisk together the bananas, eggs and melted butter. Gently fold the flour into the banana mixture, and add the chocolate (and nuts and/or cinnamon or cardamom, if using).

Arrange paper cups in a muffin tin, and spoon in the batter until a centimetre from the top. Bake large muffins for 30 minutes and smaller ones 20-25 minutes. The muffins are ready when you press the top of one and it bounces back slightly. If still gooey, bake 5 minutes longer. Don't over-bake, as they will sit in their own heat and continue to cook after you take them out of the oven. Leave to cool in the tin for at least 30 minutes.

Berry Buttermilk Muffins

Berry muffin is a favourite all around the world, so of course I wanted it on the menu at Small World. And, as expected, it's a big hit! I like using buttermilk here because it adds a hint of freshness. It's essential to keep the batter light and fluffy, much more so than with the banana or carrot muffin recipes.

Ingredients

250 g (9 oz) plain (all-purpose) flour
150 g (5 ¹/₂ oz) caster (superfine) sugar
1 ¹/₂ teaspoons baking powder
¹/₂ teaspoon bicarbonate of soda (baking soda)
¹/₄ teaspoon fine salt
2 eggs, beaten
250 ml (9 fl oz) buttermilk
115 g (4 oz) butter, melted
100 g (3 ¹/₂ oz) mixed fresh or frozen berries
1 teaspoon vanilla extract

Method

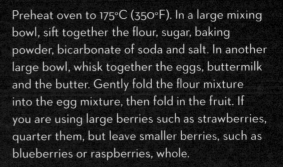

Preheat oven to 175°C (350°F). In a large mixing bowl, sift together the flour, sugar, baking powder, bicarbonate of soda and salt. In another large bowl, whisk together the eggs, buttermilk and the butter. Gently fold the flour mixture into the egg mixture, then fold in the fruit. If you are using large berries such as strawberries, quarter them, but leave smaller berries, such as blueberries or raspberries, whole.

Arrange paper cups in a muffin tin, and spoon in the batter until a centimetre from the top. If you are using frozen berries, scatter them on top of the muffins. Bake large muffins 30 minutes, smaller ones 20-25 minutes, or until golden brown. The muffins are ready when you press the top of one and it bounces back slightly. Leave to cool in the tin for at least 30 minutes.

Lemon Poppy Muffins

Make as *Berry Buttermilk Muffins*, but omit the fruit. Instead, fold poppy seeds gently through the mix before spooning into the muffin cups, and then add a generous dollop of our lemon curd, which we use in our *French Lemon Tart* (see recipe, page 154) into the middle of the muffin before baking.

Carrot and Apple Muffins

WITH TOASTED SEEDS AND COCONUT

This is probably my favourite muffin, and it's packed with goodies. It's a perfect between-meals snack, not super-sweet, but just tasty and full of ingredients to keep you going for a while!

Ingredients

400 g (14 oz) plain (all-purpose) flour

200 g (7 oz) caster (superfine) sugar

2 teaspoons bicarbonate of soda (baking soda)

2 teaspoons ground cinnamon

1/2 teaspoon ground ginger

1/2 teaspoon fine salt

125 g (4 1/2 oz) carrots, peeled and grated

1 large apple, grated

35 g (1 1/4 oz) dried coconut, shredded

3 large eggs, lightly beaten

150 ml (5 fl oz) sunflower oil

2 teaspoons vanilla extract

150 g (5 1/2 oz) mixed seeds (we use sunflower, sesame and pumpkin)

Method

Preheat the oven to 175°C (350°F). In a large mixing bowl, mix together the flour, sugar, bicarbonate of soda, cinnamon, ginger and salt. Stir in the grated carrot and apple, and the coconut. In a second bowl, beat together the eggs, sunflower oil and vanilla extract. Add this to the flour mixture and stir well. Fold in the seeds.

Arrange paper cases in a muffin tin and spoon in the batter, not filling the cases all the way to the top. Bake for 30 minutes, or until a toothpick inserted into the centre of a muffin comes out clean. Remove from the oven and leave in the tin for 30 minutes. This gives the muffins time to cool, otherwise they will break apart.

So, now that you have our recipes, it's time to throw your own parties.

You can mix and match the recipes any way you like, of course, but you'll find a few of our own favourite combinations on the following pages. The dishes work well together, and never disappoint. The servings are generous, for we think it's better to have more, than to have disappointed friends. This way, your guests can have doggy bags to take home–there will be no complaints about that!

Menus serve 12. Prior to each recipe you'll find the number of times we suggest you multiply it.

Spring Garden Party

1 x Spanish Tortilla with Sweet Potato

1 x Thai-Style Fish Cakes with Salmon and Cod

1 x Sun-Dried Tomato and Green Olive Tapenade

2 x Spicy Broccoli and Pumpkin Salad

2 x Mediterranean Couscous Salad with Fresh Herbs

1 x Our Legendary Carrot Cake

1 x Berry Buttermilk Muffins

Summer Picnic

2 x Sandwiches:

Chicken Pesto with Grilled
and Marinated Veggies

Special Tuna with Avocado, Wasabi
Mayo and Rocket

Goat's Cheese with Balsamic
Onions and Rocket

2 x Beetroot and Apple Salad in a
Toasted Cumin and Orange Dressing

2 x Roasted Fennel, Feta and Kalamata Salad

2 x Haricots Verts Salad with Roasted Walnuts
and Parmesan Shavings

1 x Cookies (your favourite from
the cookie options)

1 x Muffins (your choice from the
muffin selections)

Autumnal Festivity

3 x Carrot Ginger Soup

1.5 x Aussie Beef Pies

1.5 x Portobello Mushrooms with Sweet Potato and Taleggio

1.5 x Beetroot and Apple Salad in a Toasted Cumin and Orange Dressing

1.5 x Spicy Broccoli and Pumpkin Salad

1 x Pecan Pie

1 x French Lemon Tart

Wintery Sunday Lunch

3 x Spicy Coconut and
Parsnip Soup

3 x Chicken Fillet in a Mustard
Cream Sauce

3 x Mediterranean Couscous
Salad with Fresh Herbs

3 x Haricots Verts Salad
with Roasted Walnuts and
Parmesan Shavings

1 x Classic New York
Cheesecake

1 x Rich Fudge Brownies

The Recipes

Thank You!

Making this book has been a wish of mine for several years. This could never have been accomplished on my own.

It all starts with the recipes. A big thank you first of all to Ray Keisen, who worked in Small World for over a decade, and also to Zoe Painter Gottehrer and Salka Hamar Penning. They all tweaked the recipes in their own way and introduced their favourites as well.

I would also like to thank the staff, past and present for their loyalty, enthusiasm and hard work.

Making a book is very much like making a recipe. Only here the ingredients are people. I like to use good ingredients and I was lucky to find good people who were equally passionate about making a delicious book.

Thank you to Salka Hamar Penning for the wonderful photography and for being a sweetheart.

A huge thank you to Hélène Lesger for making this book happen, and giving it her own personal touch.

Along the way I was helped by many people especially Ayla Ryan who kept pushing me to continue.

Thank you also to Anat Geiger and Rosemary Barron for their share in getting the text right, and to Anja Timmerman from Forte Publishers who believed in this project from the get-go.

And finally thank you to my partner Clarence Yssel for his contribution to this book, and most of all for always being there.

DISCARD

Published in 2017 by Murdoch Books, an imprint of Allen & Unwin
First published in 2016 in the Netherlands by Forte Uitgevers BV, Baarn

Murdoch Books Australia
83 Alexander Street, Crows Nest
NSW 2065
Phone: +61 (0)2 8425 0100
murdochbooks.com.au
info@murdochbooks.com.au

Murdoch Books UK
Ormond House, 26-27 Boswell Street,
London WC1N 3JZ
Phone: +44 (0) 20 8785 5995
murdochbooks.co.uk
info@murdochbooks.co.uk

For corporate orders and custom publishing contact our
business development team at salesenquiries@murdochbooks.com.au

Text © Sean Wainer 2016
Photography © Salka Hamar Penning, Atlas Panther Photography, Amsterdam

Publisher: Corinne Roberts
Cover Design: Madeleine Kane
Photography: Salka Hamar Penning, Atlas Panther Photography, Amsterdam
Editors English text: Rosemary Barron, Barbara Luijken, Kay Delves
Graphic design and lay-out: Egbert Clement, Studio Jan de Boer, Amsterdam
Image manipulation pages 6-7, 86, 188: Stephan Lesger, Amsterdam
Project coordination and editing: Hélène Lesger, Books, Rights & More

All rights reserved. No part of this publication may be reproduced, stored
in a retrieval system or transmitted in any form or by any means, electronic,
mechanical, photocopying, recording or otherwise, without the prior written
permission of the publisher.

ISBN 978 1 74336 950 0 Australia
ISBN 978 1 76052 755 6 UK

A cataloguing-in-publication entry is available from the catalogue of the National
Library of Australia at nla.gov.au
A catalogue record for this book is available from the British Library

Colour reproduction by Splitting Image Colour Studio Pty Ltd, Clayton, Victoria
Printed by 1010 Printing International, China

IMPORTANT: Those who might be at risk from the effects of salmonella poisoning
(the elderly, pregnant women, young children and those suffering from immune
deficiency diseases) should consult their doctor with any concerns about eating
raw or lightly cooked eggs.